Speaking Our Faith

*Equipping the Next Generations
to Tell the Old, Old Story*

KIT CARLSON

Church Publishing
NEW YORK

Church Publishing Incorporated
Editorial Offices
19 East 34th Street
New York, NY 10016

Cover design by: Jennifer Kopec, 2 Pug Design
Typeset by: PerfecType, Nashville, TN
Printed in the United States of America

A record of the book is available from the Library of Congress.

ISBN: 978-1-64065-027-5 (pbk.)
ISBN: 978-1-64065-028-2 (ebook)

I Love to Tell the Story

I love to tell the story
Of unseen things above,
Of Jesus and His glory,
Of Jesus and His love.
I love to tell the story,
Because I know it's true;
It satisfies my longings
As nothing else would do.
I love to tell the story;
'Twill be my theme in glory.
To tell the old, old story
Of Jesus and His love.

—Hymn 64 in *Lift Every Voice and Sing II*
Words: A. Katherine Hankey (1831–1911)

To Andrew and Katie

Acknowledgements

This book grew out of my doctoral project at Virginia Theological Seminary, where I was able to transform my angst over the future of the church and the "decline of the nones" into an experience that has brought me hope and joy. I have to thank—first and foremost—David Gortner, who was director of the Doctor of Ministry program at that time, and whose work with young adults and whose work on evangelism has deeply informed mine. Also, much love and gratitude to my thesis advisor, Lisa Kimball, and the thesis readers, Tim Sedgwick and Al Johnson. And many thanks to Al Johnson for bringing me out on the road to further develop Speaking Our Faith with the clergy of the Diocese of Northwestern Pennsylvania.

The best support network *ever* was my doctoral cohort—Rachel Nyback, Diane Vie, Ketlen Solak, Jenny Montgomery, and Mary Hudak. We are FOUR forever.

The vulnerability, commitment, and courage of the post-Boomers whose stories are told in this book have been an inspiration to me. I am particularly grateful to the members of the very first Speaking Our Faith group—Blake, Lisa, Kelly, Abigail, Alejandro, Mike, Natalie, Julia, and Cherie—whose names and identifying details have been changed, but whose very real selves and spiritual lives are dear to me. Later, I trained leaders for more Speaking Our Faith groups, and they took this program to its next level. Thanks to Becky Beauregard, Chris Thomas, Jo Hartwell, Gerardo Aponte, and Matt Penniman. I am deeply appreciative of those who nudged this project along—Chris Yaw, who pestered me to turn Speaking Our Faith into a class for his ChurchNext online learning school, and

Nurya Love Parish, who told me the first time we ever met to get going and get this book out there.

For all their love, support, and encouragement, I am grateful first, for my husband, Wendell Lynch, as well as the people of All Saints Episcopal Church in East Lansing, Michigan. And to my own Millennial children, Andrew and Katie, who are not active in church anymore, I offer thanks for challenging me to learn more about the reasons church might no longer have meaning for you and your peers.

Finally, Sharon Ely Pearson at Church Publishing has been a gentle, encouraging, and insightful editor. And a shout out to copy editor Tess Iandiorio, because copy editors toil behind the scenes and get very little credit, and I want to remedy that fault.

Kit Carlson
September 1, 2017

Contents

Introduction

The church is constantly renewing itself with each generation, and we are either part of that renewal or part of standing back and letting it fall. So it almost feels like a "trust fall" exercise for the church. The church is constantly falling into the arms of the next generation of people who are catching it.

—Mike, a father of two in his mid-30s

The church is taking a "trust fall" into the arms of that next generation, but the numbers of arms extended to catch it are dwindling. The rapidly changing American religious landscape is one of growing secularism. People who might once have been nominally Christian are walking away from church in dramatically increasing numbers. With this growing indifference to religion, the Church can no longer assume that there is religious cultural literacy in the United States. And all the research points to people under age forty as the primary demographic drivers of this drift from religious faith and practice.

Across America, religious affiliation is declining. Every time a new research study on American religion is published, it reveals a growing number of "nones," people who express no religious preference. In 2015, Pew Research Center put the percentage of unaffiliated at almost 23 percent,[1] a percentage that had risen significantly in the previous decade. While churches of all varieties—including Catholic and evangelical churches—are losing members, the Protestant mainline has taken the hardest hit. "In 2007, there were an estimated 41

---

1. "America's Changing Religious Landscape," Pew Research Center, May 12, 2015, http://www.pewforum.org/2015/05/12/americas-changing-religious-landscape/ (accessed January 27, 2017).

million mainline Protestant adults in the United States. As of 2014, there are roughly 36 million, a decline of 5 million," Pew Research Center reports.[2] And the Episcopal Church is suffering those same losses: average Sunday attendance in the domestic church declined more than 26 percent between 2005 and 2015.[3]

Younger adults are driving the decline. One-third of Millennials—people born between 1982 and 2004–identify as atheist, agnostic, or nothing in particular, and that percentage is still growing.[4] The faithful, church-attending generations that built and filled churches in the 1950s and 1960s continue to die away; they are not being replaced by new, younger church members. By any measure, our "trust fall" is a perilous one.

But there is a new energy afoot in the Episcopal Church these days that perhaps will help to break our fall. There is a sense that the Spirit is moving, drawing us into a movement of love and reconciliation that can change the world—into the Jesus Movement. Presiding Bishop Michael Curry has reminded the church that we are part of the Jesus Movement, and we follow a loving, liberating, and life-giving God into deeper relationships with God, one another, and creation. In a video he made shortly after his consecration in 2015, Curry told the church, "Now is our time to go. To go into the world to share the good news of God and Jesus Christ. To go into the world and help to be agents and instruments of God's reconciliation. To go into the world, let the world know that there is a God who loves us, a God who will not let us go, and that that love can set us all free."[5]

2. *Ibid.*
3. "Average Sunday Attendance by Province and Diocese, 2005-2015," The Episcopal Church, http://www.episcopalchurch.org/files/average_sunday_attendance_by_province_and_diocese_2005-2015.pdf (accessed March 17, 2017).
4. Pew Research Center, May 12, 2015.
5. The Public Affairs Office of The Episcopal Church, "Presiding Bishop Michael Curry: This is the Jesus Movement and we are The Episcopal Church, the Episcopal Branch of the Jesus Movement," The Episcopal Church, http://www.episcopal church.org/posts/publicaffairs/presiding-bishop-michael-curry-jesus-movement -and-we-are-episcopal-church (accessed March 19, 2017).

Evangelism is moving front and center. There have been evangelism conferences, and even revivals (!) across the wider church. Evangelism is one of the three main priorities of The Jesus Movement in our church, with four audacious objectives: *Inspire* Episcopalians to embrace evangelism; *Gather* Episcopal evangelists; *Equip* all to be evangelists; *Send* all as evangelists.[6] The purpose of this kind of evangelism is much larger than simply a "church growth" project—although the hope is that as people hear the Good News, they will want to grow in faith in community with others. There is a bigger purpose to evangelism—sharing what God is doing in the world. The point is to "listen for Jesus's movement in our lives and in the world. Give thanks. Proclaim and celebrate it! Invite the Spirit to do the rest."[7]

This is easier to write on a website than to put into practice. Bishop Curry has called Episcopalians "God's shy people," and for this, and a variety of other reasons, it has not been the practice in our church—or in most mainline Protestant churches, either—for members to speak freely about their faith. And so a bridge must be built: between the ingrained reticence that most faithful members feel, and the joyful ability and desire to speak about faith. Before we can speak evangelically, sharing the Good News of how Jesus is moving in our lives and in the world, we have to get comfortable speaking about Jesus in the first place.

I understand it can be hard. That is why I wanted to help "God's shy people"—like those in my own parish—learn to speak about faith with confidence and conviction. And I knew the focus had to be on the fugitive generations that are walking away from faith, on those younger adults under age forty. So I began to explore this phenomenon—the "rise of the nones"—and to ponder how to approach the problem in an average congregation. This became the

---

6. "The Jesus Movement," The Episcopal Church, http://www.episcopalchurch.org /page/jesus-movement (accessed March 19, 2017).
7. *Ibid.*

focus of my research for my Doctor of Ministry degree at Virginia Theological Seminary. I wanted to understand *why* this is happening. Where are the young people going? Why have they walked away from church, and what might be done to reach out to them, listen to them, and perhaps speak to them about Jesus in a way that might bring them home? How can we help the younger adults who still *are* in church to reach out to their peers, their friends, and colleagues, and share the joy and meaning they find in their Christian faith? How can we *inspire, gather, equip,* and *send* evangelists into the rising population of younger adults who are "nones"?

These questions led me on a journey that resulted in an experiment—to use "sacred conversations" with younger adult Christians between the ages of twenty-one and forty to help them learn to speak about faith in a small group setting. I had hoped that this kind of dialogue would equip them to speak about faith to their peers who do not share their faith. I did not anticipate the power that conversations like these can have. From the first session, it became clear that people really do want to talk about faith, but at the same time they are wary—many barriers get in the way of being able to speak freely about what one believes and the faith one practices. But by the end of the initial five-week conversation group I started with mainline Christians under forty, I was convinced. Safe conversations about faith *can* foster the ability to share faith outside of the safety of that group. They can help younger adults to start to evangelize.

It is important for every generation to speak about our faith with clarity, passion, and conviction. And as my zeal for cultivating these kinds of conversations has continued to grow, I have used this model with people of varied ages and life experiences. Since that first experiment, the guided conversations I dubbed "Speaking Our Faith" have been expanded into the wider membership of my congregation. Five leaders learned to facilitate these conversations and fifty of my own parishioners—ranging in age from twenty-three to eighty—have participated in these guided dialogues. Some of them even asked for a second round, so I added a new session of "Speaking Our Faith 2.0." I have shared this process with members of my own diocese (Michigan) and the Diocese of Northwestern Pennsylvania, and adapted it for an online course with ChurchNext.[8] I have written this book and the accompanying Leader's Guide to share my learnings with the wider church, because I believe that to speak authentically about faith—to "always be ready to make your defense to anyone who demands from you an accounting for the hope that is in you" (1 Pet. 3:15)—is a vital aspect of following Jesus.

As you read this book, you will find places where the data, the forces in play, and the reasons it is so hard for us to talk about our faith with others, all can apply to people of any age and any generation. It's important for us to look honestly at this material and see how it applies to us, regardless of whether we come from the Baby Boom generation or are a member of Generation Z (the post-Millennial generation). Our failure to commend the faith that is in us has contributed, in a very large part, to the decline of the modern mainline church. All of us need to become more comfortable and more adept at sharing our faith. The process of the Speaking Our Faith program can work for anyone who desires to do that.

But while sharing our faith is important for *all* Christians, it is going to be crucial for the younger adults in our churches who are catching the church as it makes that "trust fall" across the generations. For those younger adults who are leading the charge in religious disinterest and disaffiliation, finding their way to faith is going to happen through encounters they have with their peers in the wider world, not within the walls of a church. They are not going to seek out the church—the church needs to reach out to them. They will need to really see why a life of faith is meaningful, why it's worth it. They will need to hear about the love of God from their friends, from people their own age who *do* believe, and who are willing and able to

---

8. www.churchnext.tv/library/speaking-our-faith/about/ (accessed July 19, 2017).

say why. Speaking Our Faith is one way to equip our faithful younger adult members to speak about faith to their non-believing friends.

This book describes how my foray into "sacred conversations" with adults who are under forty illuminates the challenges facing the church in the twenty-first century. It also offers some glimpses of hope for ways the church might begin to address those challenges. And the *Speaking Our Faith: Leader's Guide* will help you to try it too—to get the faithful young adults in your community of faith to start talking, first to each other, then to their friends and family members. Speaking Our Faith can also be used to help older church members to get better at talking about faith, making it a much less terrifying and much more manageable prospect than they might have believed. Some of the barriers to talking about faith are the same for anyone in our mainline churches, regardless of age.

In Chapter One, I outline the challenges facing American churches in the twenty-first century, and look at how the "rise of the nones" has manifested in mainline denominations like the Episcopal Church. We will meet "nomads," "prodigals," and "exiles"—younger adults who are disinterested, disengaged, or just barely holding on to their life of faith. But we will also meet "reclaimers"—younger adults who have found a new life of faith in traditional, liturgical congregations.

In Chapter Two, I explore the barriers to speaking about faith. Some of them apply to mainline Christians of any age—most of us were never taught or encouraged to speak about faith. But there are barriers specific to the generations born after 1965, a result of a rapidly changing society, the birth of the internet, and the increasingly diverse and multifaith world they inhabit. *Vulnerability, not having all the answers,* and *being able to speak one's own truth* are key factors that affect the ability to speak comfortably about faith.

In Chapter Three, we meet the members of a Speaking Our Faith group—nine Christians under age forty who gather to learn to put words to their experience and understanding of God. Finding God in the story of one's own life is where they begin, and the chapter investigates ways that personal narrative and autobiography can help believers begin to tell their own chapter of God's "old, old story."

Chapter Four describes how the group members begin to develop their own theologies and personal ethics. The modern secular culture does not ensure that people will automatically absorb the principles of Christianity, and the chapter shows how dialogue can help people come to "ideological consciousness," as Mikhail Bakhtin would term it, or "owned faith," in John Westerhoff's model of faith development. In a postmodern world, where truth is considered to be relative, how can faithful younger adults claim the truth of Christianity for themselves?

In Chapter Five, the group gathers for the final time to share their own statements of faith, based on the Baptismal Covenant found in the Episcopal Church's Book of Common Prayer. The power and practice of testimony—writing a statement of faith and speaking it out loud—can lead to more comfort in speaking about faith. Walter Brueggemann's work helps to show how testimony can be an authentic practice for mainline Christians, who might not be comfortable with the bold proclamations of their more evangelical brothers and sisters.

It doesn't end there. In Chapter Six, the Speaking Our Faith participants head out to have conversations about faith outside of the safety of the group, with family members or friends who do not share their faith. New understandings of evangelism can help "God's shy people" honestly adopt evangelism as a practice, with their parents or children, with their friends, and with their wider circle of colleagues.

While sacred conversations may not be the magic bullet that will end the "rise of the nones" and solve all the evangelical problems of the modern church, they provide a place to begin to speak. Before anyone can evangelize, there has to be a basic comfort and confidence in speaking about faith. These guided conversations can provide the grounding that is necessary to begin forming evangelists in our own tradition, people who can speak about the loving, liberating, life-giving God in ways that are authentic, honest, and true. The church is already falling into the arms of those younger adults who *do* believe. The future of the church depends on their ability to speak boldly. We must equip these younger generations—along with the generations of their parents and grandparents, and also the generation following them, that of their children—to find both the words and the confidence they will need if they are to proclaim the ancient faith of Christ in an increasingly secular age.

A Note on Terminology

This book is concerned mostly with adults between the ages of twenty-one and forty years old. This age group has been termed "younger adults" by Robert Wuthnow, and "post-Boomers," by Richard Flory and Donald Miller. I use these terms interchangeably. All of these researchers have noted similarities in the generations that follow the Baby Boomers, and so lump them together with these descriptors. While there is some disagreement among sociologists on the exact starting and ending dates for the post-Boomer generations, I use the dates set by William Strauss and Neil Howe: Generation X falls between 1961 and 1981, and the Millennial generation falls between 1982 and 2004. Thus, most of my work is focused on Millennials and the younger range of Generation X.

It is important to remember that the oldest members of Generation X are now in their early fifties. Although my work focuses on people under forty, it can be extrapolated up to people age 55 and younger. This means the forces that affect these generations' participation in faith communities—and their ability to speak about their faith to others—cover the bulk of adults below the age we might term "senior citizens." These adults are distinctively different from Boomers and their parents.

CHAPTER ONE

A Whole New World—
The Rising of the "Nones"

Not long ago, at a party in my neighborhood, I fell into conversation with a couple in their late sixties, members of a large, historic, mainline denomination church in the heart of the city. They have loved their church for more than forty years, been faithful contributors, and have grown in their own faith and commitment to Christ. And yet, "Our church is struggling," they told me. "We don't know if we can stay open. Our membership is shrinking, and our utilities alone are $80,000 a year. We don't want to close, but we don't know what is going to happen next."

What they are experiencing in their own unique church setting is a phenomenon going on across America; as church attendance declines, church membership drops, and many churches struggle to remain open or even eventually close. "The Rise of the Nones," *Time* magazine named it in 2012, as data poured in from Pew Research, Barna Group, the Public Religion Research Institute, and others. Religious affiliation among Americans is declining rapidly. And that decline is particularly pronounced in the post-Baby Boom generations, those adults under fifty years old from Generation X and the Millennial generation.

Anxiety about these trends abounds in every denomination and in most congregations. Whether that anxiety is fueled by tense congregational meetings, as once-prosperous churches struggle with insufficient budgets, or whether that anxiety is ramped up by bitter blog posts and self-replicating angst across social media, American Christians are wondering what to do about the "nones" and also the "dones" (those once-faithful church members who have simply walked away), and what the future holds for their congregations in particular, and American Christianity in general.

I, too, have watched these trends, and wondered how they would play out in my own context. As the rector of a midsize church in a university community in the Midwest, my long-stated goal had always been to help this congregation proclaim the gospel with its life and witness in such a way that it would be able to hand on this parish—its work, worship, witness, and ministry—to the next generation of leaders. But when I shared my goal with a colleague one day, she turned to me and asked boldly, "What if they don't want it? Seriously. What if this parish, as wonderful as it may be, is not what they want? What will you do then?"

I took her question seriously. *Would* they want it, those upcoming generations? Did they want it, even now? So I began to study this phenomenon, starting with my own congregation. I began by taking a close read through our membership database. As I counted each family—adults and children—I began to notice how many of the "young adult members" were absent. Most of the young adult children of the congregation's active members no longer attend my parish or any other church.

Then I looked back through the parochial reports for the whole life of my more-than-sixty-year-old parish. Parochial reports record congregational membership, baptisms, monetary giving and the like, and provide the data used by the Episcopal Church as a whole to chart its membership and giving trends. As I looked at the decades from 1956 forward to today, I did see an uptick of growth late in the twentieth century. My parish's highest peak of membership since the early 1960s was during the "baby boomlet" of the late 1980s and early 1990s, the years when these now-young-adults were in Sunday school. That boomlet ended in the mid-1990s, which means that the last children of that cohort have moved beyond even college age. They are now officially adults.

These boomlet children, also called "Millennials," are more unaffiliated from religion than any generation before them—at the same age. The 2015 Pew Research Center demographic study, "America's Changing Religious Landscape," reported that 36 percent of young Millennials (born between 1991 and 1997) were unaffiliated, as were 34 percent of older Millennials (born between 1982 and 1990). And the number of "nones" among the older Millennials had grown by nine percentage points since 2007.[1] Those who had grown up with no religious upbringing were remaining unbelievers, and many who had been brought up in a religious tradition were abandoning it.

In 2010, The Pew Forum on Religion and Public Life reported that "the large proportion of young adults who are unaffiliated with a religion is a result, in part, of the decision by many young people to leave the religion of their upbringing without becoming involved with a new faith."[2] And the rise of the unaffiliated will have a cumulative effect, because the more religiously unaffiliated people there are, the more religiously unaffiliated people there will be. In 2014, Pew Research Center noted that two-thirds of Millennials raised

1. Pew Research Center, May 12, 2015.
2. Allison Pond, Gregory Smith, and Scott Clements, "Religion Among the Millennials," The Pew Forum on Religion and Public Life, February 17, 2010, http://www.pewforum.org/Age/Religion-Among-the-Millennials.aspx (accessed September 4, 2011).

unaffiliated remain that way into adulthood. "Unaffiliated" has a better retention rate than any religion in America.[3]

But will the wandering younger adults who *were* raised in a religious tradition stay away for good? Won't they come back when they begin to pair up, get married, and have children? This is a commonplace argument among church leaders and older Christians—the belief that if we just wait it out, the young families will return to church when they settle down, just as their parents and grandparents did. Unfortunately, the data does not support that hope. Sociologist Robert Wuthnow did a sweeping demographic review of the place of religion and faith among younger adults in his book *After the Baby Boomers: How Twenty- and Thirty-Somethings Are Shaping the Future of American Religion.* And part of that demographic review outlines the role that marriage and childbearing play in religious participation. Wuthnow discovered that marriage is an especially strong corollary for church attendance—along with having children. And the likelihood of attending church does increase with each child added to a family. However, fewer people are marrying at all any more, and those who do, marry much later.

Life events and societal forces will tend to draw young people back to church as they settle into adult life. But, as Wuthnow points out, the forces in play for these young adults are much weaker than they were for their parents' and grandparents' generations. The current trend to postpone marriage and child rearing can delay church participation until these adults are at least in their early forties. By then, many of them have been out of church for twenty years or more, adding inertia as another hurdle to be overcome in the return to religious practice and church membership.[4] "For many, the prover-

3. Michael Lipka, "Millennials Increasingly Are Driving Growth of the 'Nones,'" Pew Research Center, May 12, 2015, http://www.pewresearch.org/fact-tank/2015/05/12/millennials-increasingly-are-driving-growth-of-nones/ (accessed February 4, 2017).
4. Robert Wuthnow, *After the Baby Boomers: How Twenty- and Thirty-Somethings Are Shaping the Future of American Religion* (Princeton, NJ: Princeton University Press, 2007), 62.

bial lessons of faith learned at their mother's knee may be powerful enough to sustain their interest in religion until the circumstances of their lives again make it convenient to participate," Wuthnow writes. But for those who have wandered from church and then go through decades of life outside a church community, finding it easy to live unconnected to faith, he warns that, "religious organizations will simply be less relevant for many than was true in the past."[5]

Why do so many younger adults walk away from church in the first place? It may be born in the rebellious spirit of the years following high school, when students relish a chance to sleep late on Sunday mornings, even as they start to test the family values they learned at home. It may be exacerbated by a long "emerging adulthood" period, in which post-Boomers push-off marriage and parenthood until they are well into their thirties. But sociologist Michael Hout also believes something deeper is affecting the faith of the post-Boomers—the "think for yourself" attitude of their Baby Boomer parents. "Many Millennials have parents who are Baby Boomers, and Boomers expressed to their children that it's important to think for themselves—that they find their own moral compass," he told Pew Research Center. "Also, they rejected the idea that a good kid is an obedient kid. That's at odds with organizations, like churches, that have a long tradition of official teaching and obedience. And more than any other group, Millennials have been and are still being formed in this cultural context. As a result, they are more likely to have a 'do-it-yourself' attitude toward religion."[6]

I hear this commitment to independent choice and this hesitation about faith, even in the voices of the post-Boomer parents in

---

5. *Ibid.*, 70.
6. David Masci, "Q and A: Why Millennials are Less Religious Than Older Americans," Pew Research Center, January 8, 2016, http://www.pewresearch.org/fact-tank/2016/01/08/qa-why-millennials-are-less-religious-than-older-americans/ (accessed February 3, 2017).

my parish. I rarely hear—in fact, I may never have heard—a young parent say to me, "I hope my child grows up to love Jesus and to love the Episcopal Church like I do." Across the board, the parents of children in my congregation say, "I want my children to choose their faith for themselves. I don't want to tell them what to believe. I just want them to have a grounding so that they can make up their own minds about religion."

Those now-grown children have done just what their parents intended. They made up their own minds about faith. And all the data surrounding those decisions supported what I was observing in my own parish. The Millennial children of still-active Baby Boom members were walking away from church. And few of them held out any hope to their questioning parents and clergy that they were planning to come back.

What Happened? Where Did Our Children Go?

> But opposite the place of the cavern
> They wrote the story on a column,
> And on the great church-window painted
> The same, to make the world acquainted
> How their children were stolen away
> And there it stands to this very day.
> —from "The Pied Piper of Hamelin" by Robert Browning

Robert Browning's poem tells the story of a medieval village overrun by rats. One day a mysterious piper appears, and for a great fee of a thousand guilders, agrees to rid the town of rats. He plays, the rats follow, fall into the river, and drown. But then the mayor of the village refuses to pay the fee, so the piper takes his revenge. He starts playing a new tune, and all the village children start following him. He leads them up the hillside, where a giant cavern appears in the rock. They all enter the cave, the mouth of the cave closes behind them, and the children of the village are never seen again.

For Baby Boomer parents entering their senior years, and for the older generations ahead of them who still faithfully fill the pews, it can seem like a piper has passed through our churches and charmed our adult children away. And in the local congregation, it's usually not clear—to their clergy or their parents—where they have gone and why. But those researching the "rise of the 'nones'" have been eager to explore the reasons young adults are turning away from faith and from the church. After all, the research shows that these younger adults' belief in life after death, heaven, hell, and miracles is as strong as their elders', and their level of prayer is the same as young adults' of previous generations at the same age. Clearly, their interest in spiritual matters has not dwindled.[7]

Why do they leave? The raw data draws a general picture: in 2012, the Public Religion Research Institute reported that 23 percent—the largest percentage of people who have abandoned the faith of their childhood—left because they stopped believing in God and church teachings. Another 16 percent left because they had problems with organized religion, and 11 percent had a bad personal experience with church or said they just "grew out of it."[8]

But other social scientists have tried to draw more rounded portraits from the data and from their own research. Christian Smith has followed young people's faith journeys from adolescence into young adulthood, using the longitudinal data from the National Study of Youth and Religion. He has sorted the young adults from that study into six religious types. Forty percent of them fell into the first three types: indifferent to religion, disconnected from religion, or actively hostile toward faith. Of the remainder, only 15 percent were

7. Pond, et al., 2010.

8. Amelia Thomson-DeVeaux, "Complicating Our Views of the Religiously Unaffiliated," Public Religion Research Institute, January 14, 2013, http://www.prri.org/spotlight/complicating-our-view-of-the-religiously-unaffiliated/ (accessed February 3, 2017).

committed to a particular faith. The other 45 percent were either selective adherents—who customized faith to fit their lives—or were spiritually open, not professing any faith, but who were mildly receptive to spirituality.[9]

David Kinnaman of the Barna Group looked at "spiritually homeless" young adults. These were people eighteen to twenty-nine years old who were raised in the Christian faith but who had either walked away or who were struggling with faith. In his "You Lost Me" project, he sorted them into three types. *Nomads* have walked away from church, but they still consider themselves Christian. They see themselves as personally connected to God or Jesus, but they don't feel the need to belong to a church or even to have Christian friends. *Prodigals* have lost their faith. They no longer describe themselves as Christian. Either the beliefs of Christianity no longer make sense to them, or else they had a bad experience that turned them off church for good. *Exiles* still feel invested in faith and church, and they still attend church. But they don't find that church or faith makes much of a connection to their daily lives. They feel stuck or lost between church and the wider culture.[10] These three types of "spiritually homeless" young adults describe those who have grown up in all sorts of Christian churches—evangelical, Catholic, and even mainline Protestant denominations like the Episcopal Church.

The "Spiritually Homeless" Tell Their Stories

Hearing younger adults' stories can help us understand why those who were raised in the church as children left the church as adults. One of the most meaningful things that church leaders can do—or

---

9. Christian Smith and Patricia Snell, *Souls in Transition: The Religious and Spiritual Lives of Emerging Adults*, (New York: Oxford University Press, 2009).
10. "Three Spiritual Journeys of Millennials," Barna Group, June 3, 2013, http://www .barna.com/research/three-spiritual-journeys-of-millennials/(accessed February 4, 2017).

that faithful, aging parents of post-Boomers can do—to connect with these younger adults is simply to listen. Ask them what is happening in their spiritual journeys. What did they learn growing up in the church about Jesus and faith? What factors are contributing to their relationship (or lack of relationship) with God and the church right now? What do they imagine their relationship with religion and religious practice will be in the future? Sacred listening begins with an approach like this—letting younger adults speak for themselves about God and Jesus, and hearing them out without judgment or debate. The spiritual journeys of three "spiritually homeless" post-Boomers embody the kind of stories we might hear, if we ask.

The Nomad. Allison grew up in the Episcopal Church. Her mother was a part-time church secretary who also taught Sunday school, faithfully, week after week, year after year, throughout Allison's childhood and teenage years. And that meant that Allison was also at church, actively participating, as often as her mother. "I literally grew up in the halls of my childhood church," she said. "I was in the choir before I could even read the words on the page. I was an acolyte. I was in the youth group all the way through high school." But all that singing, all that acolyting, all those mission trips and lock-ins and group games didn't make the connection to God that her mother intended. During all those years, during all that activity, Allison never related her life in church to her relationship with God. It was "something I had to do to make my mother happy, rather than something that I did because it brought me closer to God," she confessed. "I never really felt close to God until I was out of college."

With no authentic faith of her own, when Allison graduated from high school, she was not motivated to find a faith community. So she didn't. She went to college, and then on to physical therapy school. She came home on holidays and turned up with her family for Christmas Eve services, and sometimes on Mother's Day. But she didn't show up when she was home for the summer, and she did not get involved with a church or campus ministry at school.

Now at age thirty-one, Allison is married with an infant son. She did get married in the church of her childhood, and she brought her son to be baptized there. But when she is back home with her husband and baby, Allison struggles to find a reason to go to church. She is busy with her work at a teaching hospital, and she is exhausted from the lack of sleep all new mothers know. Still, her faith in God and her relationship with Jesus feel stronger than they ever were in her growing-up years in church.

"I can't trace my 'spiritual awakening' to any one event in particular," she said. "I just decided that I wanted a deeper relationship with God. Today, I feel as though my relationship with God has never been better. I could make a boatload of excuses as to why I don't go to church on a consistent basis. I just don't. I haven't found a church that I like as much as I like my childhood church. I'm picky. And it's hard for me to say whether this affects my faith. Do I need to go to church to strengthen my relationship with God? My mother would probably say yes, but I'm not entirely sure it would change me much."

Allison fits David Kinnaman's characterization of a Nomad. She has a deep faith, but she finds no real reason to connect that faith to life in the church. She has tried attending some churches near her house, but she has not really engaged with any of them. When asked if she thinks she will ever go back to church, she said, "I really do hope I can make it a habit to attend more regularly. I want to for the sake of my children. I want to show them how important it is to have a relationship with God." But she even struggles with this notion—that raising her son in a faith community would teach him to have a relationship with God. "I know this was my parents' intention when they took me to church every Sunday, but look how far that got me."

The Prodigal. As a child in church, Giles never really liked Sunday school. But he liked everything else about the Episcopal Church his family attended. His family was deeply engaged in the life of the church—his father served on vestry and the finance committee, and his mother sang in the choir. His sisters enjoyed going to Sunday school, but Giles wanted to be in church.

"I liked actually *being* in church because I liked the idea of ritual," he said. "I enjoyed the beauty of the building, especially the stained glass, the organ, the music, the incense, when we had it. The pageantry of everything was really enjoyable for me. I remember being excited to be an acolyte. I remember avoiding Sunday school on a regular basis. I would hide in the janitor's closet or some other space to read when I was supposed to be in Sunday school. I think eventually my parents figured that out."

He didn't connect that experience to a personal faith, however. For Giles, church was about the people who were there, and the life lessons he learned from them. "I'm not sure church taught me much about faith or following Jesus, because I'm not religious at this time in my life, and I don't believe those things. But I was certainly influenced by the wonderful people that were in the church." He enjoyed listening to the sermons, and felt that the words of the priest reached him, even at his young age. He remembered when a homeless man wandered into the service one day and became disruptive, but the congregation didn't turn on the man—they embraced him. "I knew people were afraid of him, and then incredibly he became accepted," Giles said. "I really felt like there was never any pretense in that environment, and people never were competing. So I think just the lessons of treating other people with kindness, and being truly genuine were things that I took away from that place."

When he left home, Giles moved in with some friends in Brooklyn and started making his way as a jazz musician. Over the past ten years, he has had success—enough to have a stable life, a succession of gigs, and some renown as his band tours the country. There is not really space or time in his life to belong to a church, but even if there were, he wouldn't go. He lost his faith when his father died. An intense, quick-growing form of pancreatic cancer took his father's life in just six months. Giles was only twenty-six years old. "I just decided I couldn't do it anymore, and that it seemed pointless to me. I remember the day of his funeral and thinking how hollow the words of scripture rang in my ears. And I'm sure many people had the opposite reaction, but it seemed like a way of avoiding the reality of the situation and the expression of true feelings."

Giles, always an avid reader, also started to read philosophy, and the texts of other world religions. He found more reasons to walk away from Christianity. "It struck me that Christianity seemed to be a very 'selfish' religion, where everyone was focused inward. It was interesting learning about the many religions in China, which focused so much more on relationships between family members and friends. Loving others more than yourself seemed a big departure from what I'd observed in Christianity. I realize that you could argue that many of these things *are* important to Christianity, but it seemed a much different approach to me in how we focus spiritual energy." There was no spiritual energy for Giles in a Christian church. The times he did attend worship with his mother, when he went home to visit her, the sermons rang false to him, seemed empty and "vanilla." And the rhetoric of the religious right—"reinforcing the social machinery that allows institutional racism and sexism and bigotry"—drove him further from any sort of institutional religion.

Today, Giles is what Kinnaman would describe as a Prodigal from faith. While Giles could be characterized as "spiritual but not religious," even that is a stretch. The spirituality he *does* express is very much of this world. "I think I am spiritual in a way that I feel a connection with other people or when I feel overwhelmed by beauty. But I'm not really sure that I could say that I feel something that comes from anything that's not here on earth in front of me." He does not expect this will change in the future, only suggesting that perhaps he might be interested in Buddhism, if he ever did become religious.

The Exile. Chelsea grew up in suburban Baltimore, where the burgeoning influx of immigrants through the 1980s and 1990s turned the church of her childhood into a multicultural vision of the American melting pot. Anglicans from all over the world started worshipping at her formerly all-white church. "I grew up in that church at the perfect time," she said. "It was truly multicultural. We had American-born members of all races, and members who came from the Caribbean, Europe, all over Africa, South Asia, and East Asia. Since it was an Episcopal church, we had members from almost everywhere that was a former British colony. I didn't think much about the diversity at the time. The other kids were just Mary, Funke, Tisha, Jaquan, and so on. It was ingrained in me that followers of Jesus come from all backgrounds, and that the body of Christ is multicultural."

Chelsea never left the area, which remained home to her grandparents, her parents, her uncles, and cousins, all Maryland natives who stayed right where they had always lived. She attended University of Maryland and became an insurance adjuster. She was often home for family dinners, and she was often found in the church of her childhood. She served on vestry and sang in the choir and was a faithful worshipper into her early thirties. But then the church changed. Gentrification happened.

As new, young, mostly white families moved into the neighborhood and surrounding areas, the rector shifted the style of the main morning service to a contemporary one. For Chelsea, who had grown up with traditional hymns played on a pipe organ, the change was too much. While she has stayed loyal to her family's home church, she stopped attending the 10 a.m. service. She takes a ballet class near the church on Sunday mornings, and she stops by in between services to do what she considers the most important aspects of her church participation.

"I'll donate food to the food pantry, turn in my pledge, and have fellowship with the 8 a.m. congregation. It's important to me to feel connected to the community—I just don't enjoy the 10 a.m. service. I still consider myself a deeply spiritual person. I pray every night before I go to bed and every morning when I wake up. Having a faith has also sustained me at work and in my personal life. I believe that God has a plan for all of our lives. For instance, when I apply for a promotion and do not get it, I can accept that it was not part of God's plan, and that there's something better out there for me."

Chelsea is an Exile from the church of her youth. She is present—in a limited way—unhappy with what life in that community is like, but unwilling to walk away completely. She says that because the rest of her family still worships there, she probably will continue to be part of that church's life through prayer, pledging, and fellowship. But it is hard. She has thought about trying other churches, either closer to where she lives, or closer to that ballet class she has been taking. But in many ways, she is still longing for the church she grew up in. "I'd want a church with a more diverse congregation with a more traditional worship style. I don't care for contemporary music in church—I like traditional hymns. I've seen churches try to cater to younger adults by doing services with lots of contemporary music, but that's not what I want at all."

Who Are Our Younger Adults? Many Are Religious "Switchers"

There is a standard trope, or even a joke, in the Episcopal Church, that being the *via media*—a Protestant denomination with a sacramental theology—makes it a safe landing place for couples who marry outside their denomination. "I was a Catholic who married a Baptist," someone might say, "and this felt like something in between where we could both fit in." Particularly for post-Boomers who find that the church they grew up in no longer fits them theologically or politically—that their churches' stances on LGBTQ rights, the role of women, and even Biblical interpretation feel too rigid or exclusionary—the Episcopal Church's broad theology and increasingly progressive social stances make it an attractive landing place.

There *are* young adults in many of our churches. But frequently, they are not the young adults who grew up in the Episcopal Church—they have shifted away from the churches of their own childhood, finding something in this tradition and expression of faith that speaks to them.

Often these younger adults come from denominations with a high expectation for participation and belief. Catholics have been raised to believe that weekly attendance at Mass is part of believing and belonging—missing Mass is still considered a mortal sin in Catholic dogma. Evangelical Protestants have been taught that the very act of believing comes with high stakes—are you destined for eternal life or eternal damnation? When people from these kinds of traditions come to the Episcopal Church, even if they are rejecting some of their former practices or theologies with their head, the underlying rhythms, beliefs, and behaviors have been hard-wired. As they grew up, they were taught that church was important, and they carry that sense of commitment into their new life in the Episcopal Church.

They are part of a broader movement. Across American Christianity, religious "switching"—this movement in and out of religions and denominations—is growing into a larger phenomenon. No religion or denomination is only losing members, and no religion or denomination is only gaining members. There is a continual movement of people leaving and joining new faith communities, and—increasingly—abandoning those communities altogether.

The Pew Research Center's 2014 Religious Landscape Study shows a lot of churn among faiths and denominations. In Protestantism alone, the share of Americans who have switched religions is 42 per cent. But Catholicism and mainline Protestantism are losing more members than they are gaining, and the Episcopal Church is running two-for-one—two members leave for every one member who joins from another tradition. And the largest movement in this churn continues to be out of religion completely, into the ranks of the unaffiliated.[11]

Still, the liturgical and sacramental life of the Episcopal Church does attract young adults. When Richard Flory and Donald Miller started exploring the spiritual lives and religious switching of post-Boomers, they found that a significant number of post-Boomers—especially those raised in the evangelical, mega-church tradition—were turning to liturgical denominations like the Episcopal, Catholic, and Orthodox churches. They call these younger adults *Reclaimers*, people who are "seeking to renew their experiences of Christianity through the history, symbolism, and practices of ancient forms of Christianity, such as are still found in the liturgical traditions."[12] The Reclaimers tend to be college educated, often earning graduate degrees, and the ability to be people of the mind, as well as people of faith, is especially meaningful to them. "They all, in one way or another, expressed their desire to bring together the intellectual and spiritual aspects of their lives into a coherent whole . . . pursuing a spirituality that involves the whole person—body, emotions, and the mind."[13] While these young converts often express conservative social and political ideas, making Orthodoxy and Catholicism especially attractive as new spiritual homes, the deeper desire of all these Reclaimers is for both a rich, embodied, worship experience, and the close-knit, family feeling of a smaller church.

However, there has been a significant change since Flory and Miller published *Finding Faith* in 2008. LGBTQ people have become

---

11. "Chapter Two: Religious Switching and Intermarriage," *America's Changing Religious Landscape*, Pew Research Center, May 12, 2015, http://www.pew forum.org/2015/05/12/chapter-2-religious-switching-and-intermarriage/ (accessed February 6, 2017).
12. Richard W. Flory and Donald E. Miller, *Finding Faith: The Spiritual Quest of the Post-Boomer Generation* (New Brunswick, NJ: Rutgers University Press, 2008), 15.
13. *Ibid.*, 136.

widely accepted and embraced, especially by younger generations, and same-sex marriage became legal in 2015. That same year, the General Convention of the Episcopal Church authorized liturgies for same-sex marriages. Whether or not individual dioceses or congregations have completely accepted same-sex marriage, the wider denomination has staked out its position. "The Episcopal Church Welcomes You"—the statement on so much of our church signage—became a broader statement. The Episcopal Church now welcomes and affirms people regardless of their sexual identity or gender expression. For post-Boomers, this is important. Millennials—including evangelical Protestants—are far more accepting of homosexuality than older adults.[14]

This is a shift for some of the Reclaimers that Flory and Miller described. They wrote that Reclaimers tended to be politically and socially conservative, and that in seeking more ancient expressions of faith, these young people were actually shoring up their conservatism. The Catholic and Orthodox traditions continue to draw these conservative younger adults. But for post-Boomers seeking a church that welcomes their LGBTQ friends and family members—that welcomes *them*, if they are queer—the Episcopal Church offers an attractive spiritual home. They find the rich, liturgical experience that connects them to God, along with an affirming and accepting community. A young law student named Jessica is an example of one such Reclaimer.

The Reclaimer. Jessica grew up in Africa. Her Baptist missionary parents moved to Tanzania when she was five, and began to preach and teach the gospel in a majority-Muslim community. Standards were high for their family, and her parents, while loving, were strict. "There was always a sense that we were different from our Muslim

14. "U.S. Public Becoming Less Religious," Pew Research Center, November 3, 2015, http://www.pewforum.org/2015/11/03/u-s-public-becoming-less-religious/ (accessed February 11, 2017).

and Christian friends, and that we should behave better, make more sacrifices, and be more disciplined than those around us," she said.

Jessica struggled in her faith—not with the rigor, not even with the expectation that she should believe in Jesus, but with the notion that she should "feel" something. She and her brothers were assigned daily Bible readings and then at the dinner table, each of them were supposed to report what they heard God saying to them in the Scripture. "This was uncomfortable for me. I never experienced any direct communication from God." So she said what was expected of her, and she felt like a fraud. This guilty feeling of "faking it" only intensified in college. She attended a Christian university in the United States, where again, she felt like she had to "perform an emotional spirituality in front of other people." She was faking it, without ever making it.

Even though her mother told her education wasn't all that important—she was supposed to grow up to be a wife and mother first—Jessica dove in to her university studies. She was free to think and to read, and find answers to questions of faith she had always wondered about. Pope John Paul II's book *Theology of the Body* gave her an "A-ha! Moment, when I realized that you could think about the Bible systematically and intellectually, instead of relying on divine personal communication during your solitary reading." It was the beginning of the intellectual liberation of her faith.

Jessica read more Catholic writers—Simone Weil, Thomas Merton, John Henry Newman. She found that the sacramental theology of the Eucharist made sense to her. The traditional Protestant understanding of communion as a memorial service had always felt like work. "It seemed to me that all the labor of making the Eucharist meaningful fell on my shoulders, because I was supposed to summon up feelings of remembrance and thankfulness. And why were we evangelicals even bothering to do it if it was just a symbol?"

It was transformative. So transformative, that Jessica almost converted to Catholicism. The worship and sacraments of the Catholic

Church, its theology—even the role of the Pope and the Magisterium (the teaching and doctrinal arm of the Catholic Church)—all made sense to her. "The absolute assurance of the Magisterium seemed like it would make being a Christian really intellectually easy, even though I didn't agree with it on issues like marriage and sexuality." But the date for her confirmation was on Easter weekend, and Jessica had travel plans. She decided not to become a Catholic, and started attending a local Episcopal church instead.

At St. Matthew's, Jessica found many of the things Reclaimers are seeking. Flory and Miller describe five characteristics of Reclaimer longing[15]—first, they seek the ritualistic, embodied elements of liturgical churches. Jessica said, "the physicality and order of the liturgy convinced me that yes, God is definitely present in the world and loves me unconditionally. The actions of kneeling and receiving the Eucharist don't focus the attention on my worthiness to be helped, but on Christ's gift of himself to me." Second, they seek a deeper connection to the larger Christian tradition and history. Jessica loved the close attention her new parish paid to the historical church. "I learned much more about the early Church Fathers and Mothers in Episcopal homilies than I did in any history class at my Christian college." Third, they seek the support and family feeling of a small, multi-generational, religious community. "Socially, I developed close friendships with many different people because the church was active in the community. It was clear that people at St. Matthew's cared about working for justice and helping others. I was immediately drawn into working and helping in the church."

Jessica is not as rigorous in her devotional practices as many of the Reclaimers depicted by Flory and Miller. Their fourth characteristic portrays Reclaimers as people seeking strict spiritual disciplines like confession and frequent, even daily, attendance at worship. And

15. Flory and Miller, 137.

Jessica also does not fit the fifth characteristic of Reclaimers—having a desire for "religious absolutes." While she flirted with the certainty of Catholic doctrine and dogma, Jessica was happy to step into a more expansive theological and sociological world when she joined the Episcopal Church. "It was a relief to be in a church community that welcomed women to be ordained and that didn't discriminate against people because of sexuality or gender. Intellectually, I knew I was welcome to ask questions about faith, and there were always people willing to have conversations and share new books with me."

After attending St. Matthew's for a year, Jessica took the official step and got confirmed. She said, "I was so glad to receive that blessing from the bishop, especially surrounded by people who I knew and trusted." Her Baptist missionary father even attended the service. "That was wonderful. My parents have been supportive—though never unworried—about my faith decisions."

Finally, Jessica has found her way home—to the Episcopal and Anglican tradition. "I love that it's all around the world, so I know I can find communities wherever I travel. I love the tried-and-true prayers and liturgy, so I can develop my faith and love of God. I love that I don't have to extemporize my prayer and faith practices. And I know that I'm welcomed to ask questions and to dialogue with other religions and denominations."

There are post-Boomers in many of our churches. While some have grown up in the Episcopal Church and stayed, many more have found their way to the Episcopal Church from other denominations and other ways of being a Christian. Our denomination can become a home for Reclaimers and other younger adults. But the demographics demonstrate that we need to reach out to them. It's no longer an option to sit and wait for them to walk through our beautiful red doors.

There is a cartoon by Episcopal priest Jay Sidebotham that humorously highlights the futility of this approach. He calls it "A Parable of Episcopal Evangelism." The drawing is of a fish tank, with a couple of fish in it, on a beach, by the sea, next to a sign that says, "The Episcopal Church Welcomes You." The caption says: "It is likened unto an aquarium set by the ocean's edge. Any fish from the ocean are invited to jump into the aquarium if they happen to be passing by and feel like it."[16] This concept of evangelism is no longer going to work with younger adults in the twenty-first century. We must re-commit to fulfilling the question from our Baptismal Covenant, "Will you proclaim by word and example the Good News of God in Christ?"

An Urgent Question: "How are they to believe in one of whom they have never heard?"

"But how are they to call on one in whom they have not believed? And how are they to believe in one of whom they have never heard? And how are they to hear without someone to proclaim him?"

This passage from Romans 10:14 has new meaning for us today, confronted as we are by the rapid apostasy in the post-Boomer generations. As more people grow up in secular homes in an increasingly secular society, younger adults have fewer opportunities to hear the gospel story and to become disciples of Jesus Christ. But if the faith is to be passed along, generation to generation, then the gospel proclamation will require authentic voices. It will require us to respond fully to the call laid on us by scripture and the Church to "tell the old, old story of Jesus and His love."

Even in Old Testament times, believers were concerned about the transmission of faith from one generation to the next. Deuteronomy 6 tells parents to recite the law to their children and to tell them that

16. This cartoon appeared as the illustration for November in the Church Pension Group's 2016 calendar.

God freed them from slavery in Egypt, and that is why they must maintain their relationship with God. Psalm 78:4-7 says:

> We will tell to the coming generation the glorious deeds of the LORD, and his might, and the wonders that he has done. He established a decree in Jacob, and appointed a law in Israel, which he commanded our ancestors to teach to their children; that the next generation might know them, the children yet unborn, and rise up and tell them to their children, so that they should set their hope in God, and not forget the works of God, but keep his commandments.

The birth of Christianity extended that mandate to the whole world. The risen Christ gives his disciples a Great Commission: "Go therefore and make disciples of all nations, baptizing them in the name of the Father and of the Son and of the Holy Spirit, and teaching them to obey everything that I have commanded you" (Matt. 28:19-20). The early church, filled with the Holy Spirit, made new converts quickly. Even during times of persecution under the Roman Empire, Christians boldly lived and boldly proclaimed an unwavering faith in Jesus Christ. Their confident witness convinced others, and Christianity continued to grow.

Then the Roman Emperor Constantine became a Christian, and in 380 CE, Christianity was named the official religion of the Empire. And as Christianity spread from its first-century, Middle Eastern roots and became the law of every European land, the business of disciple-making became just another part of the culture. It was assumed that everyone who grew up in a Christian home in a Christian nation would become a Christian. The Christian people now lived in a religious and cultural world called Christendom.

In Christendom, civilization had both a religious arm (the church) and a secular arm (civil government). And both were assumed to be agents of Christianity. The faith of the church and the power of government were aligned, one and the same. Culturally, everyone was assumed to be a Christian and to live by Christian standards. People of other faiths—Jews, Muslims, Hindus, and others—were seen as heathen outsiders in need of conversion. The work of evangelism, or mission, was to be directed toward these outsiders living in foreign lands, not toward people close to home. Eventually, in most of the Western world, and particularly in America, being Christian got watered down to the point that it meant mostly being just a "good person" and a "good citizen."

That understanding of being a Christian is collapsing, along with the entire Christendom project. Younger adults know from experience that it is possible to be both a "good person" and a "good citizen" without any reference to a transcendent God, or to Jesus Christ. It is also obvious to any student of history that Christendom has performed acts of great evil in the name of Jesus and behaved in ways that are hardly "Christian" at all. In an interfaith world, younger generations are more willing to accept that other religions have value and wisdom to offer, which then leads them to question the truth of Christianity in such a diverse theological world. Also, post-Boomers are the first to be thoroughly reared in the postmodern era, where all meaning is relative and subjective. And so it becomes a challenge—and for many, a seemingly unimportant one—to articulate a faith that is anything more than a hodge-podge of ideas one likes or does not like.

As Christians of every denomination anxiously reckon with the "rise of the nones," many recommendations get made—to churches, to religious institutions, to clergy and other leaders—to "pay more attention" to the spiritual needs and lives of younger adults. But the emphasis in the recommendations is on changing the behaviors of institutions, not on building personal relationships. All these books, articles, blog posts, and YouTube videos tend to emphasize how churches and clergy can better proclaim, listen, invite, and include post-Boomers. And they begin to sound very dualistic, very much insider/outsider and us/them. They rarely consider that post-Boomers—the majority of whom are *not* "nones" and *do* believe in God, some of whom are even in our pews right now—might be the ideal evangelists to people in their own age group.

What would it look like if we focused on empowering and equipping our post-Boomer members to evangelize their peers? After all, Robert Wuthnow says repeatedly that "talking with friends" is an important part of the ways these younger adults construct their faith. How might faithful, mainline Christians between twenty-one and forty learn to speak of faith in such a way that their faith might inform some of these "conversations with friends"? As I developed the Speaking Our Faith program, these were the issues I had in mind. Because the apostle Paul's questions are incredibly pertinent: How *are* they to call on one in whom they have not believed? And how *are* they to believe in one of whom they have never heard? And how *are* they to hear without someone to proclaim him?

The gospel must be proclaimed, and those who would proclaim it are going to have to start to use their words.

CHAPTER TWO

Why Is It So Hard to Talk about Faith?

t's hard to put into words. How do you talk about your own faith? It's a personal relationship. *I'm defensive.*"

"The stakes are so high. There's a danger in reaching out and bringing people into your safe space."

"I wish I could tell people that you don't have to have conservative social values to be a Christian."

"My relationship to God is mine and is very private. I do not want to put my beliefs on other people."

"I don't want to come off as judgey."

"I avoid talking about my faith with people I don't know well, and I am conflicted about 'saving souls for Jesus.' What does that even mean?"

It is a struggle for young, faithful, mainline Christians to talk about faith. So many things hold them back and make them reticent and unsure. They struggle to believe or make sense of the Christian narrative. They struggle to speak of God without feeling identified with evangelists or fundamentalists. They struggle to find acceptance and to speak without judging in a world growing more religiously diverse, even as the world also grows more vocally strident and divisive. They struggle to be "out" as Christians in an increasingly secular society.

These faithful post-Boomers—Millennials and younger members of Generation X—feel trapped. On one hand, even though their faith in God is real, too often their theology is undeveloped, or else it is in radical transition. They are not sure precisely what to say about God or Jesus or redemption, and they feel uncomfortable speaking about faith when that faith is unformed and unsettled. On the other hand, they are completely terrified by the prospect of seeming like a "know-it-all" fanatic trying to save souls for Jesus. Whether or not they have experienced a more evangelical sort of Christianity—and many young Episcopalians have come to this church as an escape from evangelicalism—most of them dread angering people, making people feel judged, or worst of all, being perceived by others as right-wing Bible-thumpers, dooming people to hell.

They aren't sure what to say about God, but they know they don't want to say *that* sort of thing, and so they mostly just say nothing at all.

Sacred Conversations: A New Strategy for a Changing Christianity

The generations that follow the Baby Boomers—those born beginning in 1961—have a significantly different experience of faith from that of their parents' and grandparents' generations. The post-Boomers were the first 'latch-key' children, the first to more generally live in homes with two working parents, or with only a single parent. They were the first to have access to cable television, videotapes, home computers, cell phones, and the internet. And as they matured, the very nature of Sunday changed, and church attendance did too. Once, every business was closed on Sundays, and advertisements encouraged people to "attend the church of your choice." But blue laws died away, and Sundays became just another day for shopping or for youth sports. Church became just another option for how one might spend a Sunday morning.

But along with these more superficial factors, the entire culture and conversation around faith was shifting for these generations. In *Finding Faith: The Spiritual Quest of the Post-Boomer Generation*, Flory and Miller described five societal forces affecting religious belief and practice in these younger adults:

1. They are children of Baby Boomers, who passed their skepticism of institutions on to their children, and emphasized personal journey, without necessarily referencing institutions.
2. They live in a global community; this exposure to a diversity of people leads to tolerance and acceptance of different faiths.
3. The digital world provides rapid, global access to ideas and people with varying ideas of "truth."
4. The failure of institutions to act ethically (like the Catholic sex abuse scandals or police shootings of young black men) leads to distrust and cynicism of large institutions, like churches.
5. The rise of postmodernism has created a world with an overarching understanding that truth is what you want it to be, and you can pick what you want to think or believe.[1]

And so, as Wuthnow describes them, this cohort of younger adults has become a "generation of tinkerers," making up everything, including faith, as they go along. This tinkering trend is reflective of the stress and pull of the sorts of societal forces Flory and Miller described—including globalization and consumerism. Wuthnow says this spiritual tinkering appears in younger adults' faith lives as

---

1. Flory and Miller, 7–10.

a kind of *MacGyver*-like cobbling together of ideas about God. They are church shoppers and church hoppers, looking to music, films, the internet, and other pop-culture resources for spiritual guidance, searching for answers to existential questions in many venues beyond churches. He writes, "Spiritual tinkering is a reflection of the pluralistic religious society in which we live, the freedom we permit ourselves in making choices about faith, and the necessity of making those choices in the face of uprootedness and change that most young adults experience. It involves piecing together ideas about spirituality from many sources, especially through conversations with friends."[2]

Conversations with friends . . . in the work of Wuthnow and many others, *conversation* came up over and over again as the primary way that young adults formed their ideas about faith. As I pondered how this practice of conversation could be used to help faithful young adults share their faith with others, I remembered a sermon preached by a colleague, himself a Gen-Xer, who was raised in a non-religious family, and who came to Christian faith as an adult. He said, "During the time when I was outside the church, I met many people, both religious and non-religious, and had chances to think many things about faith, life, and God. In fact, I found many non-religious types utterly fascinating, and in many ways more accepting. Church seemed to be full of rules to obey and follow. Why would I want to go to church early Sunday morning to hear a long sermon? Could I not go to church and still feel enlightened?"

But then he found the answer to his dilemma in dialogues—he called them "sacred conversations"—with people of faith. As he talked with friends, he realized that sharing what he did *not* believe was easy, but when he had to state what he *did* believe, he struggled to find words to describe it. But over time, as he talked with Christian friends, he found new perspectives on God. He stopped

2. Wuthnow, 135.

passing judgment on religious people, and was actually drawn into faith in the process of sharing different ideas with them.

I became interested in how "sacred conversations," like those my colleague described, could help young adults define and articulate their faith. And so I developed the Speaking Our Faith program, a five-week series of facilitated conversations that lead participants from an exploration of their current understanding of the nature of God and their life of faith to the crafting of a personal faith statement. Then participants are asked to initiate a conversation about faith with a friend or family member, someone they know, but who does not share their faith.

As I have led these sessions over the past few years, as I have trained other leaders to conduct the conversations, and as I have circled back to talk to participants and leaders about their experiences, I have learned much about the forces that affect speaking about faith—particularly in the lives of post-Boomers. These are difficult times for young adults, as they try to live their faith and to speak about their faith. The rapid secularization of our culture, the diversity of religious practices, and the intensifying of divisive speech are just some of the forces in play, keeping faithful, open-minded, mainline young Christians from sharing their faith. Natalie, a participant in one of the first Speaking Our Faith groups, personified many of these difficulties.

Natalie Struggles to Talk about Her Faith

The story of Natalie embodies many of the barriers post-Boomers experience when they think about sharing their faith with other people. The day she came to talk to me about her experiences in speaking about faith, I could hear her footsteps in the hallway, her high-heeled ankle boots clicking with confident strides. Natalie always dressed stylishly, and this day was no exception: her blue polka-dot dress was insufficient for the chilly, early spring weather, but a purple wool coat with a peplum skirt provided added warmth. She had finished the Speaking Our Faith program, and then she had actually talked to someone about faith when it was done. So she sat down at my conference table with a lithe grace, ready to speak her truth, to tell me her story of how she learned to talk more comfortably about faith.

At first glance, Natalie would seem to be an articulate spokesperson for belief. Although she was only twenty-three, she was an eloquent conversation partner, using humor and metaphor to illustrate her thoughts. Faith and religion were woven through all aspects of her life—her graduate research focused on conservative religious women and fashion, and as an undergraduate, she had been a counselor at a Christian camp—until the camp director began disparaging queer people. "I quit my job theatrically because I happen to be queer myself," she said. "I came out of the closet and went through a whole year off from the church. And now I've been reintegrating myself back into that, and also into the queer faith community, to see if I can connect with the queer power of my religion."

Natalie had deep roots in a childhood wrapped in religious practice and religious tradition. But she still struggled to speak about faith. "While we went to church every single Sunday growing up—and we were related to half the congregation—we didn't talk much about it at home, and my parents didn't really extol biblical virtues at all." Her family was typical of mainline Protestants, aligning church with culture, and there was no sense as she grew up that she should ever speak about personal faith or evangelize. So Natalie shut down after an unexpected and hurtful encounter in grade school with fellow students who were from religiously rigid backgrounds. "They were spouting off values that I did not want to emulate . . . values I saw as intolerant or hateful. And so because of my condemnation of religious intolerance, all my classmates in high school thought I was an atheist. They were really surprised when they found out I went to church twice a week."

As time passed, and Natalie began to claim her sexual and political identity, her language about faith focused on social justice and LGBTQ acceptance in the wider church. And when she did "come out" in her hometown as a faithful Christian, sometimes the response was harsh: 'What church would *take* you?' "That hurt, and also was kind of exciting, to see that I was breaking that assumption for them," she said. And so she adopted stereotype-busting roles: *Queer Person of Faith. Feminist of Faith.* Even *Academic of Faith.* But at the same time, Natalie knew that she was speaking about her roles, and not about her self, not about her own faith and relationship with God. She joined a Speaking Our Faith group because she wanted to better articulate her identity as a Christian. "When I talk about the tenets of my faith, I might as well be Jewish," she explained in the first group session.

Natalie had wondered if she was just creating a faith in opposition to others' faith, picking and choosing among theologies and biblical texts as if she were cruising a salad bar. The Bible was a struggle for her. "I tried to read it cover to cover and got twenty pages in before I felt so oppressed as a woman that I quit. Well. Yeah. I tried. Gold star . . . I made an honest effort." Her church stopped youth formation programs after confirmation, and Natalie felt out of her league, with a sixth-grade Sunday school education . . . going up against biblically literate, biblically literal, believers who used the Bible to condemn her for her sexuality.

Natalie was quick to name vulnerability as a hindrance to speaking freely about the faith that touches her in her heart. She has deep wounds as both a survivor of trauma and as someone who struggles with depression and anxiety. When she drew her faith as a metaphorical house in one of the group exercises, there was a room upstairs for "storage, where I keep all the tough crap that I don't want to see the light of day, like doubt and anxiety and boxes of guilt and depression and trauma and broken bonds and things that I don't want to touch." Natalie feared the risk of self-exposure.

So when she had finished the Speaking Our Faith group and decided it was time to speak to another person about faith, it was someone she trusted, a former boyfriend—an atheist—who came over to help her get her car unstuck. They began talking about deeply personal things, and that conversation became a safe space where Natalie could speak about herself, and about God. "It felt very *vulnerable* and that was uncomfortable, to like *lay* everything out there." What she *didn't do* was talk about how the church and gender politics intersect. Instead, she talked about how she knows God. "Explaining to him how I see God and feel a calling that . . . that idea that we're all called to a priesthood of something. I feel called to a priesthood in education, through what I do and trying to listen to that voice as I'm blindly groping around in the dark, asking, 'Where is God in all this?' How I witness God in interpersonal interactions, and in transformative social justice, and in those moments of darkness and terror, where I see God."

Because Natalie hears such strong voices of judgment in her own head ("Oh, you're silently judging me right now, because I still go to church and you might think I should be beyond this."), her friend's non-judgmental, receptive listening inspired her to take another risk. She was meeting with the chair of her thesis committee—a secular, quantitative scientist—and she spoke about her faith again. "It came very naturally. It's like divine intervention. I believe in that cosmic shove. That's what was happening, like God was saying, *you need to remember and keep in mind what I am doing in your life and not be ashamed of it or shy about it.*"

As Natalie prepared to leave my office, she offered a vision of hope for her life and witness in her secular professional and personal worlds. "It's a very vulnerable and isolated position to be in—at my job, and among my friends—to be a person of faith. But I would like that to be known, I think. Especially if I can be in a position to dismantle stereotypes and make people more comfortable. I don't like proselytizing, but I would like them to have it in the back of their minds: 'Well, Christians don't suck. Natalie's here.'"

What Gets in the Way? Barriers to Speaking about Faith

American culture is rapidly becoming a secular one, and this presents an evangelical challenge to all Christians in a post-Christendom world. But it presents a particular challenge to Episcopalians, who are notoriously reserved when it comes to speaking about faith. David Gortner explains that Episcopalians have had a certain discomfort with evangelism ever since the eighteenth century, when the Episcopal Church rejected the fervor of the First Great Awakening and began to identify evangelism solely with foreign mission.[3] Episcopalians have never been consistently encouraged—either by the institutional church or by their own parish leadership—to share their faith with their neighbors. They never developed an appreciation of the work of evangelism or developed the necessary skills for it.

This Episcopal reticence around evangelism may be changing, as Presiding Bishop Michael Curry leads the Episcopal Church as its "CEO—Chief Evangelism Officer." Curry came to office proclaiming the power of the Jesus Movement: the movement of a loving, liberating, life-giving God who has a dream for this world much better than the nightmare we too often experience. But even Curry understands the barriers that hold Episcopalians back from evangelism. Speaking to Episcopal communicators in 2016, he said, "Episcopalians, we're not God's 'frozen chosen.' We're God's introverted people. And we're kind of shy and polite. That's what we tend to be as a church we're not pushy people. That's not our way, and I don't think we need to

---

3. David Gortner, *Transforming Evangelism* (New York: Church Publishing, Inc., 2008), 3.

pretend to be that. We need to be who we are. God's shy people need to share their stories in ways that are authentic to them, and that matter."[4]

And so Natalie is not alone. She is like many Episcopalians—and other mainline Christians—of every age and generational cohort, right now, in the twenty-first century. Mainline Protestant membership is declining across the board, and that is in large part because the culture of these denominations has discouraged members from evangelizing. It is not unusual for most mainline Christians to struggle to find the words, or the comfort level, or the desire, even, to speak about Christian faith, and then to come up short.

But for faithful people in the post-Boomer generations, there are even more specific barriers to speaking about faith. The taboos against publically speaking about faith are strong, emphasized by the wider culture, and also by those denominations that have neglected to foster and teach evangelism. The growth of the Evangelical movement over the last thirty years—with its cable television networks, high-profile preachers, conservative political activism, and megachurches—has crushed any desire among mainline Protestants to evangelize, because they don't want to be identified with that kind of Christianity. And the forces identified by Flory and Miller—including skepticism of institutions, tolerance of other faiths, rapid global access to a variety of ideas and "truths," and a postmodern sense that all truth is relative—all combine to make younger mainline Christians more uncertain about the validity of their faith, and much less willing to talk about it with others.

Natalie's story exemplifies most of the barriers to speaking about faith that other Speaking Our Faith participants have named:

A lack of experience in speaking of faith and a lack of support for doing so. Natalie grew up as a regular church attender with a

---

4. Michael Curry, *Address to Episcopal Communicators*, Portland, Oregon, April 21, 2016, (https://youtu.be/znYsRim8KTA, accessed December 28, 2016).

complete lack of conversation about faith at home. She described her family as only "moderately religious, but with perfect attendance." Other post-Boomers who grew up in traditional churches—where faith was supposed to come through membership in the church and through living in the wider culture, without further discussion—expressed the same disconnect.

Difficulty reading, understanding, and accepting the Bible as sacred scripture. Natalie approached the Bible like a salad bar, picking and choosing the parts she liked or could believe. In Speaking Our Faith groups, this topic erupts early on, as people unload their deep struggles with scripture and women, scripture and science, and scripture and fundamentalism, a discussion that carries on well into subsequent sessions.

A desire to be open-minded. This creates a double bind as these faithful post-Boomers reject Christian fundamentalism. Then at the same time, they express deep confusion over how they can claim their own faith without shutting out other people because of their faith or their lack of faith. "I don't want to offend anyone or lose any friends, and I think that impedes my ability to be convincing about my own faith journey," Natalie said. Abigail, a school teacher, talked about having a Muslim boyfriend and the ways they differed in what they thought about Jesus, "and I'm like, OK, if he's not the Son of God for you, fine . . . And that's really fine for me, but I can't deny that for myself."

Doubts and struggles with their own faith, whether that was over the role of scripture, the existence of evil in the world, the place of science, the nature of sexuality and faith, or the gaps in their knowledge of Christian teaching and tradition. These doubts and struggles were combined with a fear that 'real Christians' had figured all of this out, and that if they spoke, they would be exposed as outsiders to the faith. Natalie took a year-long break from church after she quit her camp counselor job, because the faith expressed by the camp director made her feel excluded as a queer person. She had to leave church in order to figure out what she really believed. For other post-Boomers in these groups, it felt like a risk to simply say out loud that they had an uncomfortable relationship with the person or idea of Jesus.

The longstanding cultural taboo against discussing "politics, sex, and religion" in polite company. Although Natalie could be a *provocateur* on these three issues, she was much less willing to expose her tender spiritual relationship with God or even sometimes to be known in the academy as a person of faith. And when Mike, a marketing coordinator, tried to have a one-on-one conversation with a colleague about faith, it died a quick and awkward death. "It was as if I had asked him about his sex life," Mike said.

The Deeper You Go, the Harder the Struggle

As I have spoken and worked with younger Christians through Speaking Our Faith groups, it has become clear that the barriers to speaking about God and religion and faith go even deeper than this. I have observed three larger, emerging themes in these conversations: *vulnerability, not having all the answers,* and *speaking one's own truth.*

In our group sessions, participants spoke whole-heartedly about the depth and reality of their experiences with God and their understanding of God's love, power, and presence in their lives. But they were also shy. It felt like taking a huge risk of self-exposure to talk with people outside the safe space of the group, because their faith came out of a deep and tender place. The relationship with God—however strong or faint, well-developed or confusing—was important to them, and so they feared being hurt by cruel or casual comments. Also, their doubts and questions, their struggles with scripture, and their desire to be open-minded and not to offend someone else left them *vulnerable* to attack or rejection.

This same desire to be open-minded, along with their struggles with scripture and their doubts and questions, revealed that they did *not have all the answers.* When so much was still unclear in their own minds, it became difficult to speak coherently and confidently to others about faith. What were they to make of the inherent contradiction between a faith that makes profound truth claims, and their own postmodern sense that all truth is relative? Participants struggled to resolve the tension between the two. Some also worried that if they did not have their faith sorted out in their own minds, they could not comfortably speak about it with anyone else.

Finally, they struggled to *speak their own truth.* Even though they wanted to say something about God, Jesus, church, or prayer, they felt stymied by the cultural taboos around speaking of faith, combined with their own inexperience. Even for those from more evangelical backgrounds, the practice of testimony—of telling the old, old story—felt dangerous, even icky, and for some, just impossibly beyond imagining.

For Kelly, a busy, stay-at-home mom of three children, *vulnerability* was at the heart of her struggles to speak about faith. She did not want to talk about her beliefs with anyone outside of safe, closed groups of other believers. When I asked what would strengthen her ability to speak with others about faith, she answered, "Oh my. I have no idea. I think I would have to be in an altered state. I feel very strongly about keeping it personal and private."

While this reticence might be typical for a Gen Xer like Kelly—raised in an increasingly diverse, multi-cultural, multi-faith, globally interconnected world, where any truth is relative and open to question—it came out of a much deeper space for her. Like many in her generation, Kelly was the child of divorced Boomer parents. Her father, a rigid Southern Baptist, and her mother, an atheist, divorced when Kelly was very young. Her mother did not provide Kelly with any religious upbringing beyond sporadic attendance at the Unitarian Universalist church, and she was always quite clear to Kelly that she did not believe in God. The disconnect between her parents' divergent approaches to faith kept Kelly from finding her own way to God until she was a young adult.

Surprisingly, it was her college courses that opened Kelly to God. She read studies about the power of prayer in healing, and studies that showed that people with belief systems have better outcomes in happiness, health, and intact marriages. She had always felt a connection to God since childhood, but these studies opened up the possibility that God was real, "just these little things that were kind of like, you know, how can there *not* be [a God]?" She has been trying to fill in the gaps in her Christian knowledge ever since.

But her upbringing kept her from wanting to talk about her faith with others. When she drew a picture of a 'house of faith,' it was a fortress with a giant moat and a crabby woman peeping out of the door, saying, "What do you want??? Go away!!!" She later explained, "That castle's there for a reason." Kelly's father always condemned her mother for her atheism, and after they divorced, he would tell his young daughter that her mother was going to hell for not believing.

Kelly began to cry when she told this story. "I don't know why he would do something like that. But I was always like, my thing was, how can there be a God that condemns good people?" She paused to wipe her face and eyes with a tissue. "So that was a very deep-seated fear, and you know, at the time, it was just my mom and me. I'm an only child. So that was terrifying, and still is, I think."

In the intimate conversations of Speaking Our Faith, a sense of *vulnerability* emerged quickly. There was a belief that speaking about faith might open them to attack—bringing not only the discomfort of conflict, but also the very real fear that it would not be their ideas under assault, but their very selves. Damage might be done: to relationships, to the other's opinion of the believer, even to the believer's own sense of self-worth and security. The cost of speaking of faith—only to expose one's vulnerability—crushed any interest in talking about faith.

Brené Brown researches vulnerability, shame, and courage, and she defines vulnerability as *uncertainty, risk,* and *emotional exposure.*[5] She claims that vulnerability is at the core of all human emotion, and that people close off and shut down because they are afraid that the costs of exposure may be too high. She says we reject vulnerability because we associate it with bad feelings: fear, shame, and disappointment. In her research, Brown has found that vulnerability is the flip side of shame. She says that shame is fear of disconnection, that what we've done or failed to do can make us believe we are unworthy of that connection. Shame is an "intensely painful feeling or experience of believing that we are flawed and therefore unworthy of love and belonging."[6]

Many of the group participants described being afraid of experiencing shame: the shame of being *exposed* as a person of faith, the *uncertainty* around one's faith and the inability to articulate it, the *risk* of caring that much about God and one's spiritual life, as well as the *risk* of being labeled as one of "those"—evangelists, street preachers, judgmental authority figures, haters. To feel shame is to feel disconnected, Brown says, and the desire to stay connected, to feel loved, to feel like we belong, causes us to fear and avoid shame. It makes the act of speaking of faith seem like a vulnerable and dangerous thing. It causes us to create great fortresses with deep moats and cranky doorkeepers, so that we might stay safe and unassailed.

Not having all the answers about faith created difficulties for a young man moving from a fundamentalist religious childhood to the more liberal theology of the Episcopal Church. As a child, Alejandro used to go with his parents around the streets of his city in Peru, knocking on people's doors and telling them how to believe in Jesus Christ and be saved. He used to preach and teach in church. His

---

5. Brené Brown, *Daring Greatly: How the Courage to Be Vulnerable Transforms the Way We Live, Love, Parent, and Lead* (New York: Gotham, 2012), 34.
6. *Ibid.,* 68.

parents had him earmarked as a future pastor in their Evangelical denomination.

Then something went awry. He entered high school, then college in the United States, and he began to come to terms with his sexual identity as a gay man. "I stopped talking about faith. I wouldn't talk to people about faith issues, because my own faith was becoming different from the church I belonged to, and I wanted to respect people in their faith communities or whatever philosophy of life they had, and I just didn't want to engage."

It was a traumatic time for him, changing the smooth, easy-flowing river of his life into a torrent of rapids, with one great big waterfall—right at the end of college. "The Holy Spirit in my life did not look like the people around me, right? And obviously that meant that something was wrong with me. And God wasn't answering." And so Alejandro went over the falls and accepted his sexual identity, regardless of the teachings of his childhood faith, and his life was forever changed . . . including his life with God. "I know there was a place for God, but first he was there in the way I am supposed to understand him, then he wasn't there in the way I was supposed to understand him. And so now I'm trying to figure out if he was really there, and I'm asking questions."

An issue that continually arises in these sacred conversations is the sense that *not having all the answers* is a problem. Christianity makes profound truth claims. But a postmodern frame of reference says that all truth is relative. And so, post-Boomers struggle to resolve the tension between the two. And in addition, the kind of discomfort they feel also comes from the way they have experienced their Christian faith and what they have been taught—or have not been taught—that Christianity means.

For younger adults coming from more doctrinaire traditions, abandoning the certainty of confessional statements and Biblical inerrancy for a more expansive and progressive Christianity can feel liberating and exhilarating. But sorting out what they believe *now* is not as easy as just listing what they don't believe *any more*. While they are often Biblically literate, they are no longer biblically literal, and they begin to wonder what to do with the whole question of scripture. On the other hand, post-Boomers raised in a more progressive denomination, like the Episcopal Church, often feel ignorant in comparison with these biblically-literate peers. Most of them attended Sunday school of some sort, but few of them continued any formal course of Christian formation after confirmation—which was as early as sixth grade for some, and no later than high school for others. And they are afraid to say anything at all about faith to more conservative Christians, because they fear they will be out-argued by people who read and study the Bible regularly. Finally, some of these post-Boomers are people who came to faith with no previous religious upbringing at all, like Kelly. They have discovered God, somehow, some way. They know they believe. They may love the faith community they have landed in. But they are uneducated—or they have been erratically educated—in the very basics of Christianity.

The process of participating in sacred conversations through Speaking Our Faith helped to make these younger adults more comfortable with this ambiguity. Once they realized other people didn't have all the answers either, they made a kind of peace with their own doubts, ignorance, and questions. Sharing their uncertainty, understanding that none of them had all the answers about faith, and realizing that all of them had some doubts or struggles was very reassuring to participants. The practice of speaking and being heard with non-judgmental acceptance helped them to know that it was possible to experience these kinds of conversations without being shamed or rejected. They became more comfortable with *not having all the answers.*

Brené Brown's research shows that people who accept vulnerability, and who are shame-resilient, are people who have also accepted the ambiguity and uncertainty of life. *Not having all the answers* is so key to this whole-hearted approach to life that it is number five in

Brown's list of guideposts for whole-hearted living: *Cultivating intuition and trusting faith: letting go of the need for certainty.* Through her research, Brown "quickly learned from the interviews that faith meant . . . a place of mystery, where we find the courage to believe in what we cannot see and the strength to let go of our fear of uncertainty."[7] Speaking of faith really means being able to speak of things we are not completely certain about.

The ability to create their own statements of faith for the final Speaking Our Faith session gave the participants a place to stand, even as they accepted the ambiguity that surrounded those statements. Many of them also said that the process of sacred conversations strengthened their faith in God—using terms like "spiritual awakening" or "deepening" to describe the experience. Thus, they walked into that place of mystery where they could believe in what could not be seen, and they let go of their fear of uncertainty, just as Brown described it. Having explored and accepted their *vulnerability* and inability to *have all the answers*, they developed the confidence necessary to begin to speak about faith.

Blake, a thirty-nine-year-old husband and father of two, began to *speak his own truth* in the first session of his Speaking Our Faith group, talking with a kind of direct honesty that touched and challenged the other participants. In the first conversation session, he told the group that he had lost his job as a high school teacher and had been unemployed for the better part of a year. He didn't know what might happen to him next. And then for the remainder of the sessions, and on into his life in the congregation, Blake continued to struggle—with his past, his present, his self, his beliefs, and even with God—to speak his own truth, even as that truth developed and grew over time.

It was only after he lost his job that Blake had become more engaged in church life, tackling a variety of building projects around

---

7. Brené Brown, *The Gifts of Imperfection: Let Go of Who You Think You're Supposed to Be and Embrace Who You Are* (Center City, MN: Hazelden, 2010), 90.

the church and becoming one of the cadre of men who cook breakfast once a month. After he signed up for Speaking Our Faith, he began to really think about what his faith meant. But he didn't want to talk about it outside of the safe space of the group, or outside of the safe space of conversations with Episcopalians he knew and trusted. "From my earliest religious experiences to today, the amount I talk about faith with other people has declined. I talk about it less to people at this point in my life than at any other time. I basically never discuss it."

At age thirty-nine, Blake was solidly in the middle of the Gen X cohort, and his faith reflected many of the qualities that researchers into Gen X religion have observed. Like the Gen Xers that Jefferey Arnett and Lene Jensen studied, Blake was really living his Christianity as a "congregation of one," combining concepts and practices from a variety of traditions in individualized ways, with little to no influence from his upbringing or the formal teachings of any of the religious institutions he had belonged to.[8] And he struggled, as many post-Boomers do, with *not having all the answers*. He wondered if his individual, idiosyncratic relationship with Jesus and Christianity made him somehow not a "real Christian." He thought of himself as a "humanist who would like to be Christian, who likes the Christian story, but I'm not a 'real Christian.' I don't have the feelings and experiences that 'real Christians' have."

But being part of the group changed that for Blake. Hearing other Christians share their doubts and struggles made him feel that his doubts did not exclude him from Christianity. That his struggles with Jesus ("I'm in love with the Jesus story, but I don't know what to do with Jesus.") might actually be drawing him closer to Jesus. "Our group made me uncomfortable with that. I don't know if that's my

---

8. Jeffrey Jensen Arnett and Lene Arnett Jensen, "A Congregation of One: Individualized Religious Beliefs Among Emerging Adults." *Journal of Adolescent Research*, 17 no. 5 (2002): 451–467.

permanent state, or if it's pushing me toward being where I could pray to Jesus."

It also made him feel uncomfortable with his silence about faith. In the last conversation session, I asked the group, "What is the good news?" Blake later said that question made him feel angry, because he had created a faith for himself where he never needed to evangelize, and my question challenged that assumption. But the group conversations had stirred him up. "I've kind of had what I would call a spiritual resurgence, and that's made me think that there's a good news that needs to be passed on. Enough that it makes me feel uncomfortable that I don't like to talk to people."

One of the qualities of these post-Boomer generations is their desire for authenticity. As the first postmodern generation, Gen Xers like Blake were the first to reject universal organizing principles, dogmas, creeds, and doctrines. Instead they sought authenticity in religious beliefs, lived in day-to-day experiences. Gen Xers have been criticized for being jaded and cynical, but that cynicism arose from a too-frequent disappointment in people and in institutions that failed to meet their expectations for authenticity.[9] Millennials, their younger siblings, have become synonymous with the term "authenticity." It's all about "authenticity and Millennials," in connecting to this generation—whether it's business and marketing experts who counsel companies, or church growth consultants who urge pastors to reach out to young people.

But authenticity is not just external. These post-Boomers also hold themselves to this same standard of authenticity, of being true-to-self, honest, and coherent. Being able to *speak one's own truth* means doing that speaking in a way that is coherent with the speaker's own faith and own identity. And because post-Boomers have been

9. Richard W. Flory and Donald Earl Miller, *Gen X Religion* (New York: Routledge, 2000).

shaped by the relativity of postmodernism, their sense of integrity is not shaped by conforming their inward being to unmoving, outward standards for morality or faith, in the same way their grandparents' generation might have understood the term "integrity." Instead of seeking to align themselves with societal values, they perceive their very inner beings as under threat from outside forces of ideology and expectation. In a twenty-first century context, authenticity—a deep connection with an interior self that is always under the threat of being lost by conforming to ideas and pressures from the outer environment—has replaced integrity.[10]

This makes *speaking one's own truth* a challenge. Because the inner commitment to authenticity runs smack into the question of *not having all the answers*. To be "authentic" in speaking about faith requires more than a spoon-fed faith. As participants in Speaking Our Faith struggled with the norms of Christianity—with the Bible, with creeds, with dogmas like eternal salvation, Heaven and Hell, even with the very person of Jesus—some of this struggle rose out of their own need to claim their personal faith for themselves, to have a faith that was *authentic* to each of them. Where mainline Baby Boomers might also struggle with these same norms of Christianity, their struggle more often comes out of modernity, out of Neoclassical ideas that there is an objective truth and that faith should be aligned with objective truth. Baby Boomers wonder if the creeds are true, if the Bible has been accurately transmitted, or if the historical Jesus can be located. A post-Boomer wants to know if the creeds can be true for *me*, if the Bible can be understood as saying something about

---

10. Gil Dueck. "Inwardness, authenticity and therapy: Charles Taylor, the modern self and the implications for modern discipleship," *Journal of European Baptist Studies* 11, no. 3 (May 2011): 5–20, accessed December 30, 2016, *ATLASerials, Religion Collection*, EBSCO*host*.

God that *I* can understand, and if Jesus is someone *I* can believe in and relate to.

Breaking Down Barriers with Sacred Conversations

As participants in Speaking Our Faith begin to speak and to listen to one another in the conversation sessions, each person begins to develop their own authentic language of faith, through hammering out questions about doctrines and practices, and also by simply talking—long enough and in a safe enough setting—that it no longer felt odd or embarrassing to speak about what each of them believed or doubted.

By engaging with other group members this way, each person engages in the act of constructive theology. Constructive theology is a postmodern approach to thinking about God. It does not see theology as a system of doctrines to be learned, but as a way of constructing theological concepts to engage with the world we now live in. In *Constructive Theology: A Contemporary Approach to Classical Themes*, the Workgroup on Constructive Christian Theology describes this approach to theology: "We are not interested in merely describing what theology has been; we are trying to understand and construct it in the present; to imagine what life-giving faith can be in today's world. In doing so, as with any construction job, we are attempting to build a viable structure. In our case, that structure is an inhabitable, beautiful, and truthful *theology*."[11]

The authors describe an individual's beliefs as a sort of internal countryside, as "the complex, mental world of our deeply held beliefs about God—a rather large territory, to say the least. Next, try imagining this world of beliefs as a landscape—a vast and complex terrain

---

11. Serene Jones and Paul Lakeland, eds., *Constructive Theology: A Contemporary Approach to Classical Themes with CD-ROM* (Minneapolis: Fortress Press, 2005), 2.

holding within its borders all those images, stories, concepts, practices, and feelings that make up the sum total of 'what we believe in.'"[12] In the Workgroup's metaphor, doctrines are theological maps that describe and make sense of this inchoate terrain. In the discussion sessions, the participants become a theological cartography team, helping each other to define and delineate their own outlines of faith. Rather than exploring systematic theologies—with doctrines neatly explicated and laid out for generations to ponder and debate—the group heads out into uncharted terrain: its members' own embedded and unarticulated beliefs, where doctrines and traditions from childhood and adolescence collide with their lived adult experience, with twenty-first-century American culture, and with each individual's own struggle to live as a person of faith in a religiously confusing world.

And then, the simple act of speaking with others in a safe space about their faith and struggles also helps them to become more comfortable. Sometimes, just practicing something makes it easier. Music teachers and coaches know this, and it can also be extended to the practice of speaking about faith. In *Transforming Evangelism*, David Gortner recommends that people practice talking about faith by talking to themselves about God. "With a faith that stresses the incarnational reach of God into the gritty nature of creation itself as a habitation, talking about God should be as easy as talking about an apple, or bread, or a friend. We simply need practice."[13]

But speaking about faith is not the same as talking about an apple, or bread, or a friend, as Speaking Our Faith participants reveal when they talk about the barriers that they feel have impeded their ability to speak about faith. The possibility of experiencing shame, rejection, and disconnection from others is a very real deterrent. Some, like Blake, felt as though their faith was not valid, that they were not "real

---

12. *Ibid.*, 9.
13. Gortner, 139–140.

Christians," because they did not profess a well-structured, orthodox Christianity, and that therefore they did not dare to speak about faith.

It does take practice to talk about faith. Not just the sort of practice that comes in talking with yourself about God. We need to have these conversations with other people in order to open up new ways of thinking about God, and to sort out what we were taught to believe from what we actually can attempt to believe. And then we need to practice, putting thoughts into words, engaging those words with real human conversation partners, over and over and over again, until it feels comfortable and coherent with who we are. Creating spaces and opportunities for sacred conversation is part of the important work of telling "the old, old story."

For Episcopalians and other mainline Christians—for any of "God's shy people" of every age—the barriers that prevent us from speaking about faith are real. But for faithful, mainline, North American Christians born into the post-Boomer generations, these barriers are unique to their time, their culture, and their experiences. The "rise of the nones" presents particular challenges to these generations, because increasingly, the great number of "nones" is their peers. It is easy to say that "denominational leaders should . . ." or "churches should . . ." or "priests and pastors should . . ." do something about the growing number of unaffiliated people. But if post-Boomers discover God and assemble their spirituality through conversations with friends, then the best thing we can do—as denominational leaders, church communities, or ordained people—is to help equip our faithful, younger adult members to talk with their friends. Breaking down the barriers that prevent them from speaking about faith has never been a more important task.

CHAPTER THREE

Where Is God in My Story? The First Steps in Speaking about Faith

In 2013, Rachel Held Evans—then an Evangelical author and blogger—wrote a blog post that went viral after CNN picked it up. Called "Why Millennials are Leaving the Church," this short essay laid bare the shallowness of the methods that many churches were using to reach out to younger generations.

"Time and again," she wrote, "the assumption among Christian leaders, and evangelical leaders in particular, is that the key to drawing twenty-somethings back to church is simply to make a few style updates—edgier music, more casual services, a coffee shop in the fellowship hall, a pastor who wears skinny jeans, an updated website that includes online giving. But here's the thing: Having been advertised to our whole lives, we Millennials have highly sensitive BS meters, and we're not easily impressed with consumerism or performances.

"What Millennials really want from the church is not a change in style but a change in substance. We want an end to the culture wars. We want a truce between science and faith. We want to be known for what we stand for, not what we are against. We want to ask questions that don't have predetermined answers. We want churches that emphasize an allegiance to the kingdom of God over an allegiance to a single political party or a single nation. We want our LGBT friends to feel truly welcome in our faith communities. We want to be challenged to live lives of holiness, not only when it comes to sex, but also when it comes to living simply, caring for the poor and oppressed, pursuing reconciliation, engaging in creation care, and becoming peacemakers."

At this point, Episcopalians and other mainline, progressive Protestants might start raising their hands and saying, "Ooh, ooh! That's us! Try our church, Millennials. We've got all of that." But even though she has since joined the Episcopal Church, Held Evans proffered a plea, even a warning, that progressive mainline Christians—as well as the Evangelicals she originally addressed—would do well to heed.

"You can't hand us a latte and then go about business as usual and expect us to stick around. We're not leaving the church because we don't find the cool factor there; we're leaving the church because we don't find Jesus there. Like every generation before ours and every generation after, deep down, we long for Jesus."[1]

The post-Boomer generations may be giving up on church, on organized religion, or on a specific denomination. But hard data reveals that they are still open to a living connection to God, and to transcendent mystery, and possibly even to Jesus. Even as younger adults are abandoning the faith of their youth at a faster clip than previous generations at the same age, and even though they are not

1. Rachel Held Evans, *Why Millennials Are Leaving the Church*, CNN Belief Blog, July 27, 2013. http://religion.blogs.cnn.com/2013/07/27/why-millennials-are-leaving-the-church/ (accessed January 4, 2017).

affiliating with any other faith, their belief in life after death, heaven, hell, and miracles is as strong as their elders', and their level of prayer is the same as young adults of previous generations at the same age.[2]

In 2012, a Public Religion Research Institute study of the values of college-age Millennials noted that only 37 percent of white mainline Protestant Millennials said religion was very important, or the most important thing in their lives. However, most of the Millennials studied (54 percent) do believe in a God one can have a relationship with, and 22 percent believe in a more impersonal God.[3] They have not abandoned a spiritual life. In fact, in 2016, Pew Research reported that the number of Americans who say they often experience deep feelings of peace, as well as a sense of wonder at the universe, has actually risen—across religious traditions, and including the nonaffiliated, or "nones."[4]

However, the faith in God that these younger adults describe may not be a very robust one. They may actually be practicing what has been called "moralistic therapeutic deism" (MTD). This is a thin sort of faith in a personal God who exists mostly to help people out and boost their self-esteem. Christian Smith of Notre Dame and his fellow researchers identified it in American teenagers fifteen years ago. The teenagers they studied in the early 2000s in the National Study of Youth and Religion have grown up into today's younger adults. They

---

2. 2014 U.S. Religious Landscape Study, Pew Research Center, May 12, 2015, http://www.pewforum.org/2015/05/12/americas-changing-religious-landscape/ (accessed January 4, 2017).

3. Robert P. Jones, Daniel Cox, and Thomas Banchoff, *A Generation in Transition: Religion, Values, and Politics among College-Age Millennials—Findings from the 2012 Millennial Values Survey,* Washington, DC: Public Religion Research Institute, Inc. and Georgetown University's Berkley Center for Religion, Peace, and World Affairs, released April 19, 2012.

4. David Masci and Michael Lipka, "Americans May Be Getting Less Religious, but Feelings of Spirituality Are on the Rise," *Fact Tank,* Pew Research Center, January 21, 2016, http://www.pewresearch.org/fact-tank/2016/01/21/americans-spirituality/ (accessed January 4, 2017).

are now moving from their late twenties into their thirties—the very age group that is abandoning church at ever-increasing rates. The kind of faith they were raised with does not seem to be able to sustain them as they move into real adulthood. MTD may be partly to blame.

The "moralistic therapeutic deism" that Smith discovered "sounds something like this:

1. A God exists who created and orders the world and watches over human life on earth.
2. God wants people to be good, nice, and fair to each other, as taught in the Bible and by most world religions.
3. The central goal of life is to be happy and to feel good about one's self.
4. God does not need to be particularly involved in one's life except when he is needed to resolve a problem.
5. Good people go to heaven when they die."[5]

The kind of God these young people described in thousands of interviews is "a divine Creator and Law-Giver. He designed the universe and establishes moral law and order. But this God is not Trinitarian, he did not speak through the Torah or the prophets of Israel, was never resurrected from the dead, and does not fill and transform people through his Spirit. This God is not demanding. He actually can't be, since his job is to solve our problems and make people feel good. In short, God is something like a combination Divine Butler and Cosmic Therapist—he is always on call, takes care of any problems that arise, professionally helps his people to feel better about themselves, and does not become too personally involved in the process."[6]

---

5. Christian Smith, "On 'Moralistic Therapeutic Deism' as U.S. Teenagers' Actual, Tacit, De Facto Religious Faith," The 2005 Princeton Lectures on Youth, Church, and Culture, http://www.ptsem.edu/lectures/?action=tei&id=youth-2005-05 (accessed January 5, 2017), 47.
6. *Ibid.*, 50.

Kendra Creasy Dean was part of the research team that produced this study. Her 2010 book, *Almost Christian: What the Faith of our Teenagers Is Telling the American Church*, laid the blame for MTD on the adults in these teenagers' lives—parents, clergy, and church members—who themselves practiced a thin sort of faith that failed to communicate the traditions of Christianity to these young people and did not convince them that practicing the Christian faith was important and worth their time and energy. *We are leaving the church because we don't find Jesus there.* Rachel Held Evans has pointedly identified the void created—not only by the intolerance of the faith community she described, but also by the indifference of more progressive churches that leads to MTD.

However, when Kendra Creasy Dean went back to that same data from the National Study of Youth and Religion, she did find some hope. In youth with a passionate Christian faith, four factors emerged over and over again: They readily talked about their faith, describing a God who is "loving, powerful, and active in the world. They talked about their church communities as spiritually and relationally significant. They sensed a divinely appointed future for their lives, and they bore witness to a hopeful future."[7]

So, if we want to begin to understand, and to communicate with, and to reach these "spiritual but not religious" younger adults, these "God is my therapist and I'm a good person" younger adults, perhaps we need to start "farther back," as it were. An Inquirer's or Newcomers' class might not be where the rubber of their faith can meet the road of Christianity, and they may not be in a place where the tenets of Christian faith, or the texts of Scripture, or the liturgies of the Book of Common Prayer even matter to them—yet.

---

7. Kendra Creasy Dean, *Almost Christian: What the Faith of our Teenagers Is Telling the American Church* (New York: Oxford University Press, 2010), 40, 42. Dean notes that these committed teens were predominately Mormon, black Protestant, or conservative Protestant, but that religiously mature teens of other denominations and faiths also displayed these same traits.

Instead, we must begin where the data tells us post-Boomers live regarding faith, whether or not they are churched: in their basic connection to God and their struggles to discern how God matters in their lives and how their lives might matter to the world. Most post-Boomers are still spiritual, still believe in God, still pray, and still want to explore the difference between good and evil. But before you can catechize, you must awaken the hunger for more knowledge. And they may be ripe for a deeper exploration of questions of faith. When Christian Smith went back to those young people as they moved from teens into their early twenties, he found that MTD was losing its power. As young people grew up, left home, and moved away from their MTD-based parents, and as the crises and challenges of adult life began, their MTD lessened. "The consistency and coherence of MTD seems to be breaking down into either less or more assurance about faith in general and into either looser or tighter connections to more traditional religious faiths specifically,"[8] Smith wrote. Younger adulthood is an ideal moment to begin to try to help post-Boomers explore the power and presence of God in their lives, to help them develop more assurance about faith and tighter connections to religious communities.

This is where sacred conversations can help. They can help these faithful younger Christians to understand what they actually believe, to identify the working of God in their lives, and to begin to talk about faith—to readily talk about faith. Having these conversations in small groups also helps to build church community that can be spiritually and relationally significant. These are factors that can help build and strengthen a more committed and passionate faith in those young adult church members, who—by the grace of God—are still among us. By discovering how they can speak about the faith that is within them, post-Boomer Christians can begin to put words to their

8. Smith and Snell, 156.

understanding and knowledge of God. They can begin to find their place in the plot of the "old, old story." A portrait of one Speaking Our Faith group reveals how this process unfolds.

Learning to Speak—A Group Gathers

On a cold January afternoon, nine Christians between the ages of twenty-two and thirty-nine—some of them have already made an appearance in Chapter One—gathered in a church library for the first session of their Speaking Our Faith group. They took their places around a central square table, framed by walls of books—Bibles, prayer books, theology books, old Bible commentaries, and new devotionals—and two walls of windows looking out onto a residential street, where passers-by huddled in thick jackets against the bitter wind.

Blake—at thirty-nine, the oldest of the group—heaved into a seat, rubbing his short, almost shaved hair. His wife had regularly brought their two daughters to church over the years, but Blake himself had not been a consistent churchgoer until recently. When he introduced himself to the group, he said, "I want to think about what faith means to me, and there've been some other things that pulled me into the church in the last year, so this is kind of an extension of that journey."

Next to Blake, Natalie sat very straight as she considered the other participants with wide eyes. At twenty-two, Natalie was the youngest participant. Her modish dress and shoes reminded me that her graduate research focused on religious women and fashion. Natalie descends from a long line of Reformed Church members, and has worked for the Reformed Church campus ministry. This created a conflict when she came out as queer a few years ago. "Being in the RCA (Reformed Church of America) and working in it for so long, I have been steeped in a faith that's very Calvinist, and in my research I work with Adventists, so I have these two very different traditions," she said.

Lisa, a twenty-eight-year-old IT professional, was next. A quiet young woman with short brown hair and glasses, she had been raised in the Roman Catholic Church, but left Catholicism because it was not accepting of her lesbian identity. "I rarely talk about faith," she said, "or it's been very one-directional: someone tells you what to believe and that was it, and the conversation ended."

Alejandro and Abigail, two graduate students, came to the group as a team of best friends. They were an unlikely duo—Alejandro, a twenty-six-year-old Peruvian gay man, and Abigail, a thirty-two-year-old straight woman of Chinese descent. But they had both come to the Episcopal Church out of conservative religious backgrounds. Abigail was raised culturally Catholic in the Philippines, but wandered through Evangelical, Pentecostal, Reformed, and Wesleyan churches before finding the Episcopal Church. Alejandro is the son of prominent evangelical missionaries in Peru. His journey into America and into his own sexual identity brought him into conflict with much of his religious upbringing. He said, "I think that I need more spaces to engage in conversations about faith and what God has to say for us or for me."

Julia, a naturalist at a local park, was new to the area, still single, and seeking community. Her sense of disconnection in her new life made her seem younger than her thirty-five years. "I've been involved with lots of different types of faith communities, so trying to understand where the common threads meet the uncommon threads is the next step for me," she said, brushing back a strand of her long, ash-brown hair.

Cherie, a thirty-five-year-old, second-generation Episcopalian, is a bank manager and mother of two pre-school daughters. Her sparkling eyes and ready laugh livened the uneasy first moments of the group's conversation. Why did she agree to participate? "I feel like in the last couple of years I've done a good job finding ways to be close to God in myself, and I feel like I made some good progress. Now comes the next step . . . you can only do so much inside yourself without talking to other people and hearing from other directions."

Mike, a tall, bearded thirty-three-year-old, was the 'preacher's kid' in the group. His father had been a United Church of Christ pastor, and Mike grew up in the church. A marketing coordinator by day, his passion is singing shape-note music in a small group of like-minded amateurs. "My job is fulfilling work, but it is also draining work," he told the group. "I don't really have a place in my life to talk about faith, so here I am."

Kelly, a thirty-eight-year-old mother of three, brought a nervous energy to the table, tossing her long blonde hair and engaging eagerly in the conversation. Trained as a biologist, she had become a stay-at-home mom. "I have a strong science background, and meshing that with religion has always been important to me," she said.

These nine post-Boomers had committed to come to this room every Sunday afternoon for five weeks, to speak about faith with one another in a series of guided conversations. They agreed that when the sessions were over, they would make a stab at talking about faith with someone they knew, but who did not share their faith. By inhabiting a safe space—a holding environment where they could deeply engage questions of belief—these younger adults hoped to learn to articulate their faith more clearly and to become comfortable enough in speaking about it that they then might be able to share that faith with their peers.

Before the group began, I had asked the members to tell me something about the current state of their faith and life with God. Their answers generally reflected active lives of belief: "I'm in a place of comfort and stability with my faith." "My relationship with God and Jesus grows stronger every day." "My relationship with God is strong." But they also had questions and struggles about how one might describe God or have a relationship with Jesus: "I don't really know how to characterize my relationship with God right now (or Jesus)." "There's still a closeness, but I haven't done much to nurture it lately." "I have very undefined beliefs about my religion." "I have a lot of questions about who 'God' is."

So here were nine post-Boomers who were self-defined Christian believers (even when they struggled with the details of that belief), who did participate in church on a regular or semi-regular basis, and who were motivated enough by their desire to grow in faith that they wanted to participate in a five-week group. There was a wide diversity in their religious backgrounds, from "cradle Episcopalian" to former Evangelical, to no faith tradition at all. They all had spiritual yearnings and longings. They all had doubts and questions about God. These were not the Moralistic Therapeutic Deists described by Christian Smith, but neither were they the passionately committed Christians that Kendra Creasy Dean had identified. They were somewhere in the middle, wanting to understand God and Jesus better, wanting to focus more on what their faith was, and what that faith meant to their lives. These are the sort of younger adults we often find in progressive, mainline churches, the sort of younger adults who need some guidance so they can be equipped to speak about their faith, to understand it for themselves, and to be confident enough to be able to talk about it with their friends, family members, colleagues, and children.

These younger adults are different from adults in previous generations. While many adults in the mainline churches struggle to talk about faith, there are different reasons for Boomers' and Builders' reluctance to open up. Generations born before 1961 grew up in cultural Christendom. It wasn't necessary to speak about faith because almost everyone had some sort of connection to a faith community, even if their own relationship with God and the church was not deep or fully formed. In the mainline, it has always seemed more important to belong to a church community than to have a personal relationship with Jesus. There is also a deep strain of classism in our denomination— people will say openly that it is "tacky" or somehow "low-brow" to try to talk about Jesus or faith with other people. While there is overlap across the generations in some of the barriers to sharing faith, younger adults who now live in a multicultural, post-Christendom America have other struggles in speaking about faith that are distinctive to their place and time, as I explained in Chapter Two.

Where Is God in MY story?

In the Speaking Our Faith groups, the first real attempt to speak about God and faith comes after an exercise at the end of the first session. It invites participants to imagine their lives as rivers, with rapids, pools, twists and turns, and then to draw that river of life, looking for places where God was present or absent at key moments.[9] "The Bible is people trying to figure out what God is doing with them," I said to the group, when it reconvened for the second conversation session. "In some sense your life is your scripture as you look back on it and try to figure out what God is doing with you." I asked them to talk about their experience with this exercise, what happened when they looked at their life as a river journey with God.

Julia was the first to speak. "There are a lot of things I haven't thought about or I have avoided thinking about, particularly painful things. What I realize is that a lot of these things, like feeling God's presence or feeling God is absent . . . a lot of that comes through other people, the way they treat me or interact with me. Over the past several years, it's been a process of learning to trust myself and my gut instincts rather than believe what other people tell me is true."

Kelly said she had a powerful spiritual awakening when her children were born. "They don't tell you when you have children how terrified you feel and how you become completely vulnerable. I had my life together, then I had a child, and everything I knew went off the grid. And it was terrifying. God has always been with me, but I

---

9. Taken from Joyce Ann Mercer, *Girl Talk, God Talk: Why Faith Matters to Teenage Girls—and Their Parents* (San Francisco: Jossey-Bass, 2008), 135–136.

wasn't as open as I am now, because how many times in my life now do I go, 'Please, help me!' "

Lisa said she didn't think God was active in her life until she did the river exercise, and she discovered where God had showed up for her—when she came out as a lesbian to her parents. "I knew I had to tell my parents, and one day I was driving home and I got this inner strength from, I don't know where, and it filled me, and I was like, OK, I can do this."

Natalie spoke of God's absence. "So often in times of turmoil and doubts it's been like, 'Hello, where are you bro? Any time now. If you could come imbue me with that strength, that would be awesome.' But no dice." Alejandro said that while he was learning to accept that he was different from his evangelical family he experienced a "void of God . . . God wasn't answering." Mike added that there were times when he actively tried to make God stay away, times when "I have too much going on right now. I cannot pay any attention to God. I have to make things right on my own . . . Yeah, that didn't really work."

But Abigail said God was closest to her in times when she was suffering, in the times of the most stress and pain. "I am single, so it's really me and my own relationships. And the hurt and pain that come with relationships are mostly the major ones. I remember being so *vulnerable*, being helpless, but then feeling this immense sense of *strength and power* because I know that he's with me. But when things are flowing along fine, I feel like I'm kind of ignoring God."

Then I asked them—as they looked at their lives, what resources did they use to interpret these experiences of God's presence or absence? Where did they learn to recognize whether it was God or not? Some said nature, or music, or poetry, or even a challenging encounter in a college class. Some talked about trying to logically think their way to God, or by meditating in order to tune into the sense of obligation that is their conscience. But conversation also was important. Cherie mentioned growing up in church and then "being able to go home and talk to your parents and question and challenge and try to get some of your own head around the things that you're hearing." Julia said it was being able to talk to good friends, lifelong friends, "who can listen to you because they know your whole story and remind you of things that are important to remember."

But none of them mentioned the Bible. So I observed, "The Bible is one of the ways we know God, and we have talked about nature and music and friends, but I haven't heard any of you say you go to the Word. When is Scripture helpful, and when is Scripture not helpful? What kind of authority is it in your life, and does it help you understand who God is?"

While Abigail was quick to identify the link of music—psalms or words of Scripture set to music—as helpful for her, the rest of the group immediately owned up to struggling with the Bible. For a book that seems to offer so many Christians answers, this group found it more challenging. Kelly said it felt overwhelming. Cherie, who was raised in Sunday school and even took a "Bible as Literature" class in college, still felt lost. She said, "I can't just pick it up and just be all like 'this is nice.'" Lisa mentioned the bad images of God she received through a Catholic education, images that blocked her path. Blake said he read the Bible only so he could follow Jesus better, but not as a sacred text.

Julia, Alejandro, and Abigail—with roots in more evangelical traditions—had all read the entire Bible at least once in their lives. But Julia struggled with how the Bible had been used against women and so she, like Abigail, turned to music and the words of scripture set to tunes. Natalie confessed to reading Scripture as a "salad bar Christian." "All right, I'll take the carrots—I'll take your Christ. He's pretty cool. I'll take your peppers. I like those ideas of social justice. Not the feta cheese. I don't like the God of the Old Testament. You can take your feta cheese. But I do realize that it's disingenuous not to acknowledge that there are bits in which I see my God and bits in which I don't."

An authentic approach to helping post-Boomers identify how God is working in their lives has to honor this struggle—not only the struggle with how to use and interpret Scripture, but also the struggle with doctrines and dogmas, with church hierarchies and "how we've always done it." Because faithful younger adults who have grown up in the Episcopal Church or other mainline denominations often don't feel they understand the Bible well enough to turn to it as a resource. And faithful younger adults who have come to more progressive churches from more fundamentalist churches—while they may know the Bible thoroughly—are renegotiating and reinterpreting what they were taught about Scripture in their youth.

In his research, Robert Wuthnow discovered that a third of American younger adults believe the Bible is literally true, and most of the remainder think the Bible is divinely inspired, but not to be taken literally. "That leaves open a great deal of room for personal interpretation about what the Bible says and about how divine inspiration enters into the human realm," Wuthnow writes. He notes that this room to choose is part of the American identity—to think for yourself, to make choices about your life, your education, what products to purchase—and so it's only natural this emphasis on freedom to choose would overflow into faith decisions as well. Similarly, doctrines and traditions from various denominations are in competition with one another; for instance, what Catholics hold true in their tradition is not the same as what Lutherans hold in theirs. "Put this together with our emphasis on individual authority, and it is not surprising that some people start to distinguish between the spirituality they know from personal experience and the church teachings they hear discussed by clergy and theologians." And data bears this out. Overwhelmingly, he notes, younger adults under age forty choose personal experience over church doctrines as a way to know and understand God.[10]

This is not bad news, however. Scripture supports the spiritual practice of autobiography—looking to your own life for signs of God's

10. Wuthnow, 132, 133.

presence—and it is present throughout Christian tradition. Spiritual autobiography—learning to know and to tell your own story—is the starting point for any effective practice of evangelism.

Listening to Our Lives: Where the Spiritual Practice of Evangelism Begins

One of the main reasons Episcopalians and other mainline, progressive Christians often cringe at the word "evangelism" is because it seems so foreign to how they practice their faith, how they understand God, and how they relate to their neighbors. In these traditions, people do speak of God, but they generally do it in Sunday worship, as they pray out loud together, using set words of a liturgy that has been written by others—and as they sing together, using the music and words of hymns that have been written by others to praise God, tell stories of salvation, and bring hope and comfort. In these traditions, people don't practice personal testimony as part of their weekly worship or in their daily lives. The Church gives them their speech about God.

And then the word "evangelism" seems associated with other "sorts" of Christians, and other "sorts" of Christian faith. It feels propositional—set out a series of statements about God in order to convince someone to believe in Jesus in the same way you do. It feels exclusionary—come to faith in Christ or risk being left out at the last judgment. It feels judgmental—believe as I believe or be damned to eternal hellfire. It feels intrusive—talk to strangers about Jesus, whether or not they are interested in hearing what you have to say.

But there is another way for progressive, mainline Christians to approach evangelism—as something more personal, as a spiritual practice that can connect them deeply to God, even while they are sharing their faith with others. Approaching evangelism from this perspective begins with looking inward at one's own self and one's own story, to discover where God has been present, bringing hope out of despair and life out of death. This is important work. Because in order to be able to *speak your own truth,* you have to understand where God has been active in your own story. You have to have a clue about what God has been up to in your own life and struggles. This is the work of spiritual autobiography.

The practice of doing a spiritual autobiography is a long-standing one in Christianity, going back to St. Augustine and his confessions, and then growing to prominence in the sixteenth century as many Protestants like John Bunyan wrote the story of their coming to faith. But the work of identifying the hand of God in one's own life is also profoundly biblical. At the end of the book of Genesis, Joseph, son of Jacob (Israel), confronts the brothers who sold him into slavery in Egypt. As Pharaoh's top man, Joseph has great power to punish his brothers, who have come seeking food because of a famine. But Joseph insists that God was guiding him through his struggles, so that he would be able to provide for his father and brothers and their families when the need arose. Near the end of Genesis, when Jacob dies, the brothers still fear Joseph's revenge. They throw themselves at his feet, begging for mercy, and Joseph says the words of a person who completely understands that his life is enmeshed in God's story. "Even though you intended to do harm to me, God intended it for good, in order to preserve a numerous people, as he is doing today" (Gen. 50:20).

In John's gospel, Jesus meets a woman of Samaria at a well and begins to tell her things about her life and her relationships. She is so overwhelmed by this connection of Jesus's power to her own life story that she runs back to her village saying, "Come and see a man who told me everything I have ever done! He cannot be the Messiah, can he?" (John 4:29). Her discovery of the living water of God in the boulders and torrents of her own river of life makes the Samaritan woman an evangelist to her own village. The other villagers believed in Jesus because the woman authenticated his identity with the truth of her own biography. And in his letters, Paul continually returns to the story of his own life to explain how God is working in his ministry, and to tell the story of God's salvation. "If anyone else has reason to be confident in the flesh, I have more: circumcised on the eighth day, a member of the people of Israel, of the tribe of Benjamin, a Hebrew born of Hebrews; as to the law, a Pharisee; as to zeal, a persecutor of the church; as to righteousness under the law, blameless. Yet whatever gains I had, these I have come to regard as loss because of Christ" (Phil. 3:4b-7).

Richard L. Morgan describes the great tradition of story-remembering as central to our faith, all throughout the sweep of history, beginning with the *Haggadah* of Passover. He says the Exodus narrative is a story of bondage, liberation, and journey that is not just the story of ancient Israelites. Telling the story at Passover every year and remembering how Moses brought the Israelites out of slavery in Egypt reminds modern-day Jews that God continues to work in human history and in their very lives. Likewise, the liturgy of communion in our own churches works to connect us to the power of story. The Eucharistic prayer includes the whole human story of fall, wandering, and then, at last, our redemption by Christ. It is a prayer that centers around remembering, around those beautiful and specific words, "do this in remembrance of me." Remembering and telling the story of God's work in human lives is central to understanding the good news of Jesus Christ. As Morgan writes, "True remembering is reliving the past to give meaning to the present, and to gain hope for the future."[11]

The Power of Personal Narrative

Personal narrative can bring that past forward to the present and point onward to a larger future. Presiding Bishop Michael Curry

11. Richard L. Morgan, *Remembering Your Story: A Guide to Spiritual Autobiography* (Nashville: Upper Room Books, 1996), 21.

often tells the story of how his father became an Episcopalian. It is a story from early in his parents' lives, when they were young adults—a story they shared with him repeatedly, one that made a difference in their lives and which influences Curry's faith to this day. Curry's mother was an Episcopalian, but his father was a Baptist, preparing to be ordained as a Baptist minister. He went with Curry's mother to an Episcopal church one day, and found it very different from the Baptist church, with different hymns, the sixteenth-century language of the Book of Common Prayer, the genuflecting, sitting, standing, and kneeling. The two of them were the only African-Americans in the congregation, and that was different, too.

But the difference for Curry's father came at the moment of communion. "This was the 1940s. Jim Crow was alive and well. Segregation and separation was still the law in much of the land. The armed forces had not yet been integrated. *Brown vs. The Board of Education* had not yet taken place, and it was long before the Montgomery bus boycott. Martin Luther King, Jr., was still in seminary. Still," Curry says, "my father saw only one cup on the altar from which to drink."

His father watched as Curry's mother went forward for communion, drank from the cup and returned to her seat. And every white person who came behind her to receive communion also drank from that exact same cup. It was the power of the common cup, the moment of full inclusion, which moved Curry's father more deeply than he had ever felt before. Later he said, "Any church in which black folks and white folks drink out of the same cup knows something about the gospel that I want to be a part of."[12]

This moment—a moment at the heart of Curry's parents' lives—moved into his life and into his story as a result of their telling. It convinced him of something true about God, and something true

---

12. Michael B. Curry, *Crazy Christians: A Call to Follow Jesus* (New York: Morehouse Publishing, 2013), 58.

about the way the Episcopal tradition encounters and understands God. Curry refers to this story when he wants to explain how the power of the Holy Eucharist overcomes even the deepest estrangements. It gives him a window through which he can identify the good news, and recognize what the coming of Jesus Christ means for the world. "The gospel, the good news of God's reconciling love in Jesus Christ, can transform people and societies, despite their diversity, from the world's nightmare of division into God's intention for reconciliation."[13]

That is a powerful move, from personal narrative to evangelical speech about God's good news. Of course, Curry is particularly gifted at evangelical speech, at making these connections between life story and God's story. But he started somewhere, as we all must start somewhere, if we hope to grow in our ability to speak about faith.

The River of Life exercise used in Speaking Our Faith is one way to examine that movement of God in a person's life and journey. "Cardboard testimonials" are another, quicker way to identify a moment, a time in a person's life, when God did something powerful and transformative. I first experienced cardboard testimonials at the Evangelism Matters conference, held in 2016 by Forward Movement to help Episcopalians—God's shy people—learn more about how to share God's good news. At the conference's closing session, Stephanie Spellers, Canon to the Presiding Bishop for Evangelism and Reconciliation, handed out large sheets of white cardboard and black markers to the four hundred attendees. She introduced this exercise saying, "On one side of the card, you're going to write about something that has been a struggle for you. Just a couple of words. On the other, you capture in just a few words what God has done, where God has brought you. This is a simple way of narrating the transformation that God has worked out in your life, testifying to the truth of God's work in your life. When was there a moment when I

---

13. *Ibid.*

was at the wall, in the valley, on the ground, and God brought me out? What is that moment? How would I narrate that transformation? Write it down . . . what God has done for me," she said.[14]

She had people stand at the front of the room with samples. Each person displayed the front, then the back side of their sheet of white cardboard. *I loved money . . . now I love to give. Paralyzed by fear . . . now living confident and free. Self-centered . . . to GOD-centered. Church pew warmer . . . to mission-trip leader. 2004, marriage on the rocks . . . 2012, solid as a rock.*

Then it was our turn to write our "good news story" on the cardboard. We all did as Spellers directed, and when we were done, she invited us to turn to someone nearby and share our stories with one another. I was sitting with a former classmate from seminary. We had been friends while we were in school, but we had lost close contact over the years, and were just catching up with one another's lives at this conference. So we turned and shared our cardboard testimonials with each other. We told our stories. And even though we had known each other so well for three years in seminary, and even though we were colleagues in ministry in the church, we had never spoken to one another like that, about the way God had worked in each of our lives to bring both of us through tough, tough struggles. She had never heard my story. I had never heard hers. It took an exercise—a directed activity designed to get us to see how God had transformed our lives—in order for us to open up to each other.

It was an overwhelmingly communion-like experience. Because naturally, I felt deeply connected to her as we told each other our stories. But I also felt deeply connected to God—aware of how God has been a better friend and guide than I have ever expected or deserved—and I was filled with a profound sense of awe and

---

14. Stephanie Spellers, "Cardboard Testimonials," Evangelism Matters Conference, sponsored by The Presiding Bishop's Office and Forward Movement, November 2016, https://youtu.be/v5s_aT7fHso (accessed January 7, 2017).

gratitude. And I was in a roomful of four hundred people having the very same experience. It was a thrilling moment when they took two group photos—the first of everyone holding up side one of their cards, the second of everyone displaying the side that related what God had done in our lives. We all had seen a glimpse of God's personal, powerful, saving action.

This was evangelism as David Gortner has described it—as a spiritual practice, a way to grow in faith. "Evangelism is a willful, joyful spiritual discipline of seeing and naming the Holy Spirit at work in ourselves and those we encounter—giving voice to our own grace-filled experiences and helping others to find their voice . . . Evangelism begins most fundamentally with you."[15]

Gortner says that being able to name those moments in our lives where God was most visibly evident is at the heart of evangelism. It leads to holy listening, to becoming able to hear another person's story and learning to identify the actions of the Holy in that person's life. We have to listen to the ways God is working in our lives first, then it will be easier for us to acknowledge and point out how God is working in someone else's life. That is the starting point for any of us to be able to share the gospel—which, after all, is simply the translation of "good news."

In the initial conversations of Speaking Our Faith, the first task is to find where the good news is for each person in the group. Where has God been present and where has God been absent? Where have I been brought low in my life, slammed against the wall, but then been brought safely home? How does my story connect to the stories of the others in my group, and how do all of our life stories connect to God's great story? For these post-Boomers, these spiritual "tinkerers," their own lives are the workbench upon which they can begin to craft their theology and to construct their faith.

---

15. Gortner, 32.

CHAPTER FOUR

How Firm a Foundation: Building a Faith That Will Stand

When the Speaking Our Faith group gathered for its third round of sacred conversations, I asked them a question about God. "There's a lot we don't know about God, any of us," I said. "But what *do* you know about God out of your own experience and life and knowledge?"

Cherie jumped right in. "God is love." Then there was a long silence. Mike said, "God understands me more than I understand myself." More silence. "God is patient," Lisa offered. "God doesn't necessarily take away my suffering," Blake said. "But he gives me strength to endure, and I think sometimes God means for me to go through trials." Natalie added, "God is present in other people." Abigail said, "It's hard for me to disengage or separate God from Jesus, so I understand God through Jesus. But at the same time, I also acknowledge that God is in a lot of things that do not have the label 'Jesus' on it or

'Christian' on it. I think that's what I know now," she concluded, in almost a whisper.

And then there was a very, very long silence. "You're almost asking for our personal theologies that we've built up," Mike said. "I don't know if I could define that quickly, or easily, or clearly even. So . . ." his voice trailed off.

The group members were able to begin to *speak their own truth*, but they were stymied by *not having all the answers*. To help them find their way to words, I began to use open-ended questions. Some I had pre-planned, and others emerged as the conversation proceeded: "What else might one say about God?" "Who is the God you pray to? What's the nature, the qualities of the God you pray to?" "Let's talk about Jesus a little. How does Jesus fit into your image of God?" "Do you all believe God damns people to hell?" And finally, "We haven't even talked about the Holy Spirit, who always gets left out of these conversations."

First, they began to explore their personal connection with God. How does one know God in interactions with other people, or in the sense of presence or absence in prayer? "I think I know that I am known by God and that God *knows* me," Abigail said, in a hushed voice. "It's an exposed feeling, being known, and that's . . . that's . . . that's . . . what I know about it." Mike experienced God as multi-faceted. "There's almost a scale of how God can touch us, from the really transcendent to the very basic, fine-grained, personal, approachable," Mike said.

Then they began to struggle with the difference between the vastness of the transcendent, powerful God of the Universe and the particular, embodied person of Jesus. Jesus seemed too narrow to Cherie, and to Blake, too much to blame for many evils done in history. And even though some felt close to Jesus, the entire group resisted the exclusivity of the Christian message, that Jesus is the way, the truth, and the life, and that *no one* comes to the Father except through him

(John 14:6). This is a common sticking point for post-Boomers in a global society of many faiths. While they are very accepting of other peoples' religions, and willing to learn more about Islam, Buddhism, or even Wicca, younger adult Christians hesitate to talk about Jesus, for fear of sounding exclusionary and judgmental.

But then a few of the group members began to express a kind of envy. They longed for the certainty and fervor of people who believed Jesus was the only way to heaven. It seemed easier to them, even while they struggled with their own values—that tolerance was more important than conviction. And so Abigail asked if we could talk about hell. The group members trod the line between Blake, who was quite clear: "I don't believe in hell," and Alejandro, who struggled with the strong messages about hell from his youth. "I grew up with the idea that the pinnacle of heresy is not believing in hell, right? And when you get to that point, it's like you've abandoned everything, right? You know, you're a heretic type of Christian because it's so connected to God's justice, right?"

Finally, the group turned to the Holy Spirit. "When you say Holy Spirit, and what do I believe, one of the first things out of my mouth is 'I don't have a clue,'" Blake said. But Cherie disagreed. The Holy Spirit was so present to her that it was the clearest part of God. Abigail and Alejandro talked about a conversation they had over lunch at a local pie shop, where they spoke so deeply together about what they were experiencing in this group, that they had almost a vision. It was a deep experience of one another that was full of "the presence of God which I would name the Holy Spirit," Alejandro said. "It was that force, that experience, the part of God that helped me understand him *in the moment*," Abigail added. After everyone had weighed in, quiet Lisa spoke at last. She said that for her, the Holy Spirit is "hope—hope and understanding that all this may seem insurmountable, what you're going through right now. But there's always hope that you'll get through it."

How Does a Christian Grow?

How does anyone learn about God and Christianity, really? When Christendom existed in the Western world, it was simply assumed that people would go to church, raise their children in the church, and bring up Christians who would understand the basics of the faith. Medieval churches were full of imagery that taught the faith—statues of saints, stained glass windows telling biblical stories, crucifixes, and reliquaries. The Protestant Reformation shifted the emphasis to the Word. In the early years of Anglicanism, during the reign of Henry VIII, every parish church in England had a huge Bible chained to a lectern so that, as Bible translator William Tyndale put it, every plough boy could learn the Scriptures. Children were set to learn a catechism, to say the Lord's Prayer, the Ten Commandments, and the Apostles' Creed by heart, before they could be confirmed.

And Western culture outside the church walls—from the Middle Ages through to the end of the twentieth century—was rich with Christian story. In America, the Baby Boomers were the last generation to grow up in this explicitly Christian culture, when a child could learn about Jesus from television shows like *Davey and Goliath* and movies like *The Robe*. My own religious images in childhood were formed by the garish illustrations in the sample volume of *Bible Stories* that I found in my pediatrician's waiting room, and I remember reading billboards that said, "This Sunday, worship at the church of your choice." Even though my family was erratic in church attendance, I managed to absorb most of the biblical story just by growing up in late twentieth-century America and by being a voracious reader.

Today, the reality is that each individual American Christian has to learn the tenets of faith in their own unique way. There is no comprehensive curriculum that is universally applied across the Episcopal Church, much less across mainline Protestantism. How people are formed in faith depends on their individual life situations:

what their parents teach, what sort of formation programs their own church provides, and how often or how much they engage with the formation they are being offered. Even those raised with a strict religious upbringing can miss key parts of the message. For instance, Lisa's years of Catholic schooling left her only with an image of an almost bi-polar God who was either "nice like Jesus" or about to punish her for sinning. And for those raised more loosely—in families less focused on faith, or in families that profess no faith at all—the chances of learning the core beliefs of Christianity get even smaller.

At the beginning of this century, David Gortner interviewed eighty-two young adults (who are now young Xers or older Millennials in their thirties), people of varying class, educational levels, and social locations. And he found no consistency in these young peoples' theologies. There was no single dominant theology, and no coherence between worldview, theodicy, life purpose, and ultimate values. They were consistently diverse. And diversity within each person's set of beliefs led to diversity in their personal theologies.[1]

This is the religious world post-Boomers inhabit. And when they speak about faith, their personal theologies are as unique and unrepeatable as their fingerprints. So to help them understand and build a coherent theology for themselves—one that draws on the traditional faith of the church, but which allows them to engage their own thoughts and life experiences with that faith—it is necessary to understand how a personal theology gets constructed in the first place. In his landmark work, *Will Our Children Have Faith?*, John Westerhoff developed an image that helps interpret this process of theological construction. In Westerhoff's analogy, faith is like a tree, growing outward in concentric circles. It helps to think of faith like a tree, he says, because regardless of how many circles make up a tree,

---

1. David Gortner, *Varieties of Personal Theology: Charting the Beliefs and Values of American Young Adults* (Farnham, Surrey, England: Ashgate, 2013).

it is still a tree—whether it has one ring, four rings, or four hundred, each growing from the other in a slow and gradual manner. In the same way, faith is always faith, whether it is fresh and new or deeply entrenched over long years of believing.

Westerhoff's "tree of faith" has four rings. *Experienced faith* is at the center. This core is where the first encounter with God happens, in a community of faith that communicates the love of God to a child—or if an adult, to the new Christian. "It is not as a theological affirmation, but as an affective experience," Westerhoff explains.[2] God makes God's self known through the words and actions of the community. The next ring is *affiliative faith*, where believers find a home in a faith community that has a clear identity, and where they find a place to participate and give back. Many adults in our churches remain in the ring of *affiliative faith* their entire lives, relying on their participation in choir or altar guild, on the norms of the Book of Common Prayer and the music of *The Hymnal 1982* to sustain their faith. This can be a good thing for people like Kelly, whose faith was just beginning to find its footing. The clear support of a community with strong, authoritative teachings can keep them grounded.

But apart from Kelly, the other members of this Speaking Our Faith group were actively working through that stage Westerhoff describes as *searching faith,* which is the next circle outward. People in this circle are testing the faith as they have received it, questioning it, bringing it into conversation with others, with the world around them, and with their own experiences. This is the circle where one does not have all the answers, where one has questions and doubts, and one's faith is in flux. Then, if the struggles of *searching faith* are mostly resolved, believers can move outward, to a fully *owned faith,* the fourth ring in Westerhoff's tree. Westerhoff describes this stage as the classical Christian conversion, when "liberation, wholeness of

---

2. John H. Westerhoff III, *Will Our Children Have Faith? Third Revised Edition* (New York: Morehouse Publishing, 2012), 92.

life, spiritual health, and identity are known, and persons can live in but not of the world. The radical demands of the Gospel can now be met."[3]

But the move from ring to ring in the "tree of faith" is not a predictable journey. Where people land—and stay—depends on a variety of factors. For those in the ring of *searching faith*, who are working toward the vision of an *owned faith*, the process of conversation, of dialogue, and of sacred conversation, can help assist the movement outward. The dialogue that goes on inside a person between their own identity, the voices they carry forward from their past, and the voices of new people engaging them in conversation about God, can move a person from ring to ring to ring.

Dialogue as Deliverance—Alejandro's Story

Alejandro, who grew up as the child of missionaries, lost—not his faith, but certainly his religion, when he accepted his sexuality and owned his identity as a gay man. Fortunately, through his friendship with Abigail, he found his way to the Episcopal Church. Abigail had encouraged him to join the choir—where she had found a spiritual home—and Alejandro had been warmly welcomed by a group of people of various ages, ethnicities, and sexual orientations. It was a safe place to land for someone whose childhood faith was in tremendous flux. "I don't really know how to characterize my relationship with God right now, or Jesus," Alejandro said when he joined the Speaking Our Faith group. "It's not that I don't have one, just that I don't really know how to describe it."

But as the Speaking Our Faith group got going, things began to bubble and shift. I walked through the church building one day after the session had ended, and Alejandro and Abigail were huddled in a corner, their dark heads bent together, still talking intensely. "Oh,

3. *Ibid.*, 98.

Pastor Kit, you have started something now," Abigail said as I passed them. They looked up at me, and both had tears in their eyes.

Later, Alejandro told the group members that his experience with them had helped him decide to tell his parents that he was attending an Episcopal church. "As we had these conversations about the Episcopal Church and scripture, tradition, and reason, I was hearing other people talk about faith in a way that was expressed differently from how I was taught growing up. In my tradition, a Christian looks in certain ways and talks in certain ways and believes certain things and acts certain ways, so having that opportunity to hear other people talk about different ways . . ." gave him the impetus to talk to his parents about his shifting beliefs.

Much of that shift went on within Alejandro himself as the group conversations developed. It was a powerful experience for him to hear people with such a wide range of life experiences and a wide range of beliefs that ranged from liberal to conservative theology. "In some ways, I think maybe mine was the most conservative," he said later, after the group had ended. "And I felt good about that. Because when there were people who would say things that didn't resonate with me, or when my first instinct was to disagree, that gave me an opportunity to self-reflect. Why do I disagree so strongly? What are my bases for disagreeing? What do I believe about those bases?"

Simultaneously supported by the other LGBTQ participants and their own struggles with faith, the more liberal participants who struggled with the very person of Jesus also challenged him. When they said things like, "I don't relate to Jesus," Alejandro went back to his student group house ruminating on these questions of belief—so that when he prayed, he was much more conscious of whom he was addressing in prayer. "Like why would I sit down and say, Jesus, Lord Jesus, or Father? Why would I do that?" It helped him to encounter the Trinity more deeply, he said.

"Because of those conversations in the group, I've been able to raise some of those questions . . . what does that even *mean*, Creator of Heaven and Earth? What does it mean that he's Creator, and like, in his role?" And while Alejandro's beliefs ended up classically Trinitarian, he left with more questions than he had at the outset— about good and evil, right and wrong, sinfulness and repentance. And he realized these questions can only be worked out in Christian community. "Resisting evil is something that—as I understand God, with my community of faith—then I can understand what evil is, and what resisting evil means."

So Alejandro—who was once a child who had all the answers and was quick to tell people how they could avoid hell and get to heaven—has now become a young man who has many questions and who has learned to listen to and appreciate others' journeys of faith. Even his parents' journeys of faith. "As a result of the group, I can be less 'oh, they're so close-minded' and be more 'this is how they understand faith. This is their understanding,' and it doesn't need to be all bad. It wasn't all bad. It was positive for many people who found solace and refuge. But it was very, very exclusive of someone like me, which was bad."

When Alejandro came into the group, he was unclear about his relationship with God. But he thought he might find more clarity through these conversations about faith: "Something may change in me, something will change in me, in what ways I don't know, but it's the experience that matters, when I get to reflect and talk and learn from others." He came, as the others did, willing to engage in dialogue and conversation that could turn out to be transformative in how they might understand their faith and how they might then speak about it with others.

The power of dialogue and conversation has been unpacked in the various theories of Mikhail Bakhtin, a twentieth-century Russian philosopher and literary critic. Bakhtin believed that meaning is created in communication between people. Meaning emerges as speakers and listeners restructure concepts, reformulate them, and give them new significance. Meaning and reality are constructs that emerge through the dialogue between different voices and different individuals, each with his or her own perspective, truth, vision, understanding, and needs.

In the theories of Mikhail Bakhtin and his colleagues, dialogue is the place where one's very self comes into being. For Bakhtin, self is by nature "dialogic," and meaning emerges as different voices and different ideologies encounter and dance with one another along the boundaries between speaking and listening people. As he explains how self-awareness develops through dialogue, Tzvetan Todorov quotes Bakhtin: "I achieve self-consciousness; I become myself only by revealing myself to another, through another, and with another's help." This self-awareness is first created in our external communication with other people, who help us create a fuller picture of ourselves. But it is also created inside of us, in the internal communications we have with ourselves—with the voices, people, and teaching we carry with us in our mind and memories.[4]

But there is a deeper journey in this dialogical process, one that can move a person from *searching faith* to *owned faith*. For Bakhtin, it is not just a creation of self—it is a journey to ideological consciousness. Writing in the essay "Discourse in the Novel," Bakhtin noted that one of the problems with discourse between people is that the speech already going on in their minds complicates their dialogue. There is another level of discourse going on in each person, even while they are trying to speak and listen to one another. Each of us has many internal voices in our heads, and they are always communicating with us. In every person, there is a pre-existing background of voices, with contradictory opinions, points of view, and value judgments. And that background is always there, hanging in the mind of each listener as the speech of another approaches him. That background is always there in the mind of each speaker, too,

---

4. Tzvetan Todorov, *Mikhail Bakhtin: The Dialogical Principle* (Minneapolis: University of Minnesota Press, 1984), 95–97.

hanging in her mind as she forms and speaks a thought.[5] It complicates conversations before a word is even spoken, because there are
all these voices already speaking inside in each person. Each of us is
already listening to a unique, internal, layered language that has been
informed by our history, social location, culture, personal experiences, and prejudices.

When Bakhtin says that a person can come to ideological consciousness through discourse, he means that a person needs to bring
one's own internal language into conversation with others' speech.
In this dialogue of inner language with the speech of real-life human
beings, a person can begin to listen critically to this internal language, to test it, and to claim it for one's own. Bakhtin writes, "The
ideological becoming of a human being, in this view, is the process of
selectively assimilating the words of others."[6]

Bakhtin describes two categories of speech in play as this selective assimilation happens. There is the authoritative word—which
is the word of religious, political, and moral systems, the word of a
father, of adults, of teachers. And there is the internally persuasive
word "that is denied all privilege, backed up by no authority at all,
and is frequently not even acknowledged in society (not by public
opinion, nor by scholarly norms, nor by criticism), not even in the
legal code."[7] The struggle between these two sorts of "words" deter-
mines how an individual's ideological consciousness develops.

For Alejandro, it was the authoritative word that shaped his early
life. In his conservative, evangelical upbringing, truth was fixed and
unchanging: there was God and the devil, good and evil, redemption and sin, salvation and damnation. He knew himself, through his
salvation in Christ, to be solidly on the "plus" side of this ledger. It

---

5. M.M. Bakhtin and Michael Holquist, *The Dialogic Imagination: Four Essays*
(Austin: University of Texas Press, 1981), 281.
6. *Ibid.*, 341.
7. *Ibid.*, 342.

was only when he hit the whitewater rapids of adolescence and went over the waterfall—discovering his sexual identity and claiming it— that Alejandro had to question the terms of this ledger at all. For if this fixed and unchanging truth was, in fact, true, then the discovery of his identity as a gay man had landed him equally solidly on the "minus" side of the ledger. He was judging himself by the power of the authoritative word. Bakhtin describes the authoritative word as fixed, closed, and magisterial. It demands we acknowledge it. We encounter it with authority already fused to it. It is located outside of us, coming towards us from the past, a past that is felt to be higher. "It is so to speak, the word of the fathers,"[8] Bakhtin writes, and for Alejandro it literally was *the word of the father,* his own father: the well-known exemplar of the Christian life.

Many of the group participants had also felt the weight of the authoritative word in their lives, and it emerged in the conversations. As they struggled with the authority of scripture: "The thing that makes me the most defensive is when people say, 'The Bible says . . .,'" was a frequent refrain. As they explored the question of whether there is a hell and eternal damnation: "Maybe damnation and hell isn't what they've said it is." As they stretched to make room for other faiths, or even lack of faith, in their theological worldviews: "I have a Jewish friend who's one of the kindest, most giving people I know, but do I have to believe she's damned forever if I believe Jesus is the only way?" And as they reacted to their own religious histories, even if they were not as clear-cut or as conservative as Alejandro's: "In my church growing up, there were two images of God, the wrathful, vengeful God that knows when you sin and can come get you and punish you, and the God who created nature and is good like Jesus, and that's God too. And how do you reconcile the two?"

Bakhtin says that speaking with others can help break the log-jam created by the authoritative word. Dialogue can liberate the

---

8. *Ibid.,* 242.

other voice that speaks inside each of us—the internally persuasive word. When we enter into dialogue, the words of other human beings engage with our internal dialogue, and the voice of the internally persuasive word is awakened, so it may test the "truth" it has received against the ideas and words of others. It begins to shape its own truth, its own sense of what is good, what is true, how to be, and whom to worship. "When someone else's ideological discourse is internally persuasive for us and acknowledged by us, entirely different possibilities open up. Such discourse is of decisive significance in the evolution of an individual consciousness."[9]

Bakhtin says that this is how consciousness begins to become independent—experimenting and discriminating, as it first separates internally persuasive discourse from authoritarian, enforced discourse. Then it begins to shovel away the layers of discourse that don't matter. And over time, one's own internally persuasive discourse begins to emerge. Maybe one learns some new truths. Maybe one simply accepts that there are truths we cannot know. But the truth that emerges is truly one's own, hard won in the struggle between the "word of the father," the word of the deepest self, and the words of other people who are also struggling with their own internal voices.

This process of coming to ideological consciousness is not immediate. It happens over time. And it is a profoundly biblical experience: the journey of faith is described as "coming to believe" in both John (John 6:69, 20:29, and 20:31) and in Paul's epistles (1 Cor. 15:2, 1 Cor. 15:11, and Gal. 2:16). It is a process of coming and becoming, one that Bakhtin says carries even greater weight when it moves into the realm of theological discourse because God, "the primary subject of this discourse, is *a being who speaks* (italics mine) . . . mythological discourse does not, in general, acknowledge anything not alive or not responsive."[10] The authoritative word about God, about faith,

9. *Ibid.*, 345.
10. *Ibid.*, 351.

about the Bible, or about salvation, may seem static and inert. But the living, responsive God is neither static nor inert, something the internally persuasive word can come to honor and acknowledge.

A few months after the Speaking Our Faith group concluded, the bishop came for confirmations, and Alejandro knelt before him, received the laying on of hands, and claimed his identity as an Episcopalian, someone who relies on the three-legged stool of Scripture, tradition, and reason, someone who now values questioning, inquiry, and comfort with ambiguity. When the bishop met prior to the service with the confirmands and asked, "How many of you think you might one day have a call to ordination?" Alejandro answered that question clearly. He said, "I do."

What's It All Built Upon? Faith as a House

Most Christians of any age are not systematic theologians. The members in any one of the Speaking Our Faith groups are no exception. They are people curious about God, ready to explore their ideas about God in conversation with others, and to hash their way toward a kind of ideological consciousness or *owned faith* that works for them. Part of this process—after they tell their stories of God working in their life, after they begin to dig into their own personal ideas about God—is to help them to see where they are grounded. What is their faith built upon? What holds it up? What protects it?

One of the most transformative exercises comes between the third and fourth sessions, when participants are sent away with a homework assignment: to draw a house or a building that depicts their faith. They can ponder all sorts of questions to construct this metaphor: What rooms does it have? Are there stairs, gardens, sunny spots, scary attics? What's holding it up? What's inside? What needs remodeling? What is beautiful and homey? What is the foundation made of? Is there a roof?

The exercise sends them into the right side of the brain, the non-verbal side, where thinking is beyond words. As the participants construct a theology for themselves, they need to tap into the ways their faith actually manifests in their lives. But understanding how that faith manifests in their lives might not necessarily be easy. As the Workgroup on Constructive Theology observes, "Faith is a complex matter; like any form of life, it consists of beliefs, actions, attitudes, and patterns of behavior that are often hard to identify, much less distinguish from one another and then define."[11] And the power of faith exerts itself in many aspects of daily life, from how to apply for a job to when to take a political stand. Yet most of faith's power in an individual's life goes unremarked. "Because beliefs live deep in our imaginations, the material . . . is often more the stuff of dreams, images, memories, emotions, and all the other things that compose our daily thoughts than it is the stuff of rational concepts and philosophical arguments."[12]

So, draw it as a picture, as a metaphor. The exercise has resulted in many different approaches to this metaphor. Some people described a house they currently lived in, or the house where they grew up, and they spoke about how each room expressed a piece of their spiritual life or their understanding of God. Others described their house of faith as a ruin, a shell-shocked tumble of stones that they continually tried to set back into place. Like Kelly, some preferred the concept of a fortress, where everything they believe about God could be safely concealed behind thick walls and deep moats.

When Natalie shared her house of faith with the group, she said she wanted to draw "a very cool, Frank Lloyd Wright house. But then I remembered that I have zero visual aptitude." She went into lively detail about each room in her colorful, cartoon-like drawing, starting

---

11. Jones and Lakeland, location 360, Kindle.
12. *Ibid.*, location 383, Kindle.

with the study, where all her books on faith lived, and ending with an attic, where doubt, trauma, and other scary things were kept. I asked her, "What's it built on?" She said, "Gut feelings, and like that height of embodiment of the Holy Spirit that I witness and that I feel and experience in my spiritual life." I asked, "What holds it together?" And she said, "I feel like people around me who are the 'God with us' are what hold me together."

Abigail's house was a floor plan with a swirling hall in the center that represented her spiritual core. "That core is just the simplest, stripped-down-to-the-basics of the gospel, that Jesus died for my sins, and that's the grace and love, that's too much, that's very, very big, that I just can't forget." A living room represented community, with plenty of couches where people could gather to talk, and "also corners where there's cozy, sort of one-on-one conversations, because that really builds my faith and I do that often." A study symbolized her encounters with Scripture. There was a garden for her free, organic side: "I feel like my faith is, I just don't have to understand something before I can feel it or believe something. I'm noticing that I'm just like, 'Wheeeee! Let's enjoy the ride,' or 'Ooooh, butterflies!' "

Blake drew a massive foundation with pillars and stones. The pillars were things he was certain of, like a sense of community in church, the Lord's Prayer, and communion. The little cobblestones were things he was less sure of, like salvation, hell, and miracles. His house was surrounded by doodles—a prayer, "Carry me." That prayer keeps Blake going through his daily struggles and his long nights with insomnia. There was a sun marked "God's Holy Spirit" that outshone the drops of rain marked "Rainy Days." And then he wrote one word as a question, over and over again: "Jesus? Jesus? Jesus?"

"I have major questions," Blake said. "I have been having a major Jesus issue lately. I've been in turmoil over my thoughts about Jesus. So my house is here, and in this little house is Jesus, and I think Jesus might want to get into my house, but I'm not sure what Jesus thinks."

Orthodoxy versus Orthopraxy

It is easy for Christians to get tied up in the confusion of questions like Blake's. It is easy to worry about whether one believes correctly about Jesus, and therefore is in a right relationship with Jesus. That's because for centuries, Christians have focused on *orthodoxy*, or "right belief," as the most important factor in faith. Do you believe the correct things about God, Jesus, and the Holy Spirit? If not, you might not be a proper Christian. That has been the traditional approach to faith, and one that is still widely used.

Originally, the emphasis on correct doctrine and correct faith arose out of a need to address the many heresies that popped up in the early days of Christianity, as many different varieties of Christian faith wrestled for supremacy. After the Councils of Nicaea and Chalcedon, right belief was enshrined in creeds that outlined the bones of the faith. But then disputes over who really had the right belief began to divide Christians. In 1054, the Western Roman church split from the Eastern Orthodox church over whether the Holy Spirit proceeded from the Father *and* the Son, or the Father alone. In 1517, Martin Luther nailed his Ninety-Five Theses to the door of the church in Wittenberg, critiquing practices and doctrines of the Catholic Church. This led to the Protestant Reformation, which led to new Protestant denominations, which led to many of those denominations dividing and splitting over who believed the true doctrine, who held the true faith. It is no wonder that post-Boomers living in a multi-cultural, multi-faith society quail at the idea of articulating a faith. Because throughout history, the ways Christians have decided to articulate their faith—and demand that others follow suit—has led to dispute and division, as much as to unity and peace.

To counterbalance the problems that arise when a person tries to articulate a working orthodoxy, a focus on *orthopraxy*, or "right practice," can provide an alternative way for post-Boomers to approach faith. Many younger adults find spiritual nourishment in practices outside the church, such as yoga or meditation as a spiritual practice. Helping them to own and understand their own Christian practices as a solid ground for a Christian life takes faith out of the anxiety-provoking question of "do I really believe?" into a more expansive question of "do I really live the faith I proclaim?"

Christian practices can provide essential building blocks of faith. Diana Butler Bass has long been interested in Christian practices as a way to ground people in faith and keep churches vital. She has written extensively about the ability of practices to connect the "spiritual" and the "religious", making faith intentional. "Practices are things we do that shape who we are as they awaken us to God and others," Bass writes.[13] They are found in Judaism, Islam, Buddhism, and many other faiths—ways of praying, of offering charity, of eating or fasting, of study and learning that draw a person closer to God and help to shape him into the person God is calling him to be. And similarly, Christian practices are the things Christians do to connect more deeply to God, and to serve their neighbors, and to spread God's love into the world. "Practices shape us to be better, wiser, more gracious people now," Bass writes, "even as these very practices anticipate in our lives and communities the reality of God's kingdom that has entered into the world and will one day be experienced in its fullness."[14]

Practices incarnate doctrine. They show how people "walk the walk," instead of just "talking the talk." Bass notes that "from the earliest days of the Christian faith, Jesus's followers, known as people of the Way, were recognized by what they did—practicing hospitality and forgiveness. Too often, contemporary Christianity seems to be a religion about belief, a kind of spiritual club that can be joined by agreeing to a statement of faith. But emerging Christianity . . . is more

---

13. Diana Butler Bass, *Christianity After Religion: The End of Church and the Birth of a New Spiritual Awakening* (New York: HarperOne, 2012), 145.
14. *Ibid.*, 159.

like a recovery group: 'Act as if . . .' If you act like a Christian by joining in its practices, by following its tracings, you may well become one."[15]

In the Speaking Our Faith group, a list of practices I provided to them sparked wide-ranging conversations about faith. The list included practices like: attend weekly worship services, study the Bible, share your faith, study history of the church, pray, confess faults to others, forgive and work on healing relationships, encourage others, give financially to the church, provide hospitality to strangers, volunteer time, participate in social justice activities. As they mused on the items on the list, group members began to have sudden insights about how they were practicing their Christian faith.

Abigail realized that the house she rented with other teachers was a hub of hospitality. The international graduate students and teachers who shared her home were never homesick or lonely, and they realized it was the result of life in that house. "And it reminded me that I have that sort of mission in my life, or calling in my life, to be about healing myself and others and extending it. And when I welcome people who need healing, who will say 'yes' to my invitation, that's through community as well." "So the practice of hospitality?" I asked. "Yes, exactly," she replied.

Mike said that the practice of hospitality connected to his goal of living with integrity in his work life, as he tried to uphold Christian values in a competitive, capitalist work world. "I think, as a Christian practice, to welcome other people means to be honest with them and to be open to them and have open communication with them, even if it's not in your best interest from a business standpoint."

Blake talked about being an indifferent church attendee, but how cracking eggs at the Second Sunday Breakfast strengthened his faith—the practice of volunteering time to help. "I feel like I'm worshipping God when I'm scrambling eggs every second Sunday

---

15. Diana Butler Bass, *Christianity for the Rest of Us: How the Neighborhood Church Is Transforming the Faith* (New York: HarperCollins, 2006), 74–75.

at breakfast. I love Second Sunday Breakfast. I'm part of the church community, and I'm welcomed."

The thought that studying church history could be a practice energized Natalie. She explained how important it was to her that her family had generations-long roots in the Reformed Church, something that connected her to a very distant cousin when she visited the Netherlands. "I had no idea that was part of practice, and not just belief. Those bonds and that lineage are so vital to me, and such an important part of my faith. And that's awesome. It's just mind-blowing."

Kelly said being a Christian pushed her to observe some pretty challenging spiritual practices. Like "tithing, because giving money, that's been a bigger thing for me as opposed to just offering my time." And she also worked hard to practice forgiveness. "I'm always telling myself to forgive as Christ forgave. Fill myself with that thought. When I can, I really, really try to forgive people. Because I tell my kids to do that. Like ten times a day."

Creating a Holding Environment Where Faith Can Grow

There *are* faithful post-Boomers in church. They are there for a variety of reasons—they were brought up to attend church, they understand church as an important part of being a Christian, they want their children to have a religious upbringing, they want to be part of a faith community, and they want to continue to grow in their faith. But they are fewer in number than they once might have been, and faith communities can no longer simply assume that they are going to stick around. As Rachel Held Evans wrote, "We aren't leaving the church because we don't find the cool factor there. We're leaving the church because we don't find Jesus there."[16] When working with a

---

16. Evans, 2013.

generation of spiritual tinkerers, it is always a possibility that when they go looking for Jesus, they may be willing to seek him in all sorts of places, not just a local church.

A large minority of younger adults are such spiritual tinkerers, Robert Wuthnow explains, "church shopping and church hopping. [Tinkering] also takes the form of searching for answers to the perennial existential questions in venues that go beyond religious traditions, and in expressing spiritual interest through music and art as well as through prayer and devotional reading." Even those more traditional post-Boomers who "settle into a congregation and follow a fairly scripted pattern of prayer and Bible reading in their devotional lives . . . make choices too, and in this way are spiritual *bricoleurs*."[17]

Spiritual tinkerers can learn a lot by belonging to a faith community, engaging in its worship life, following its practices, and learning its traditions. In the right kind of church, with authentic support of older members, younger adults can find a strong holding environment that will allow them to grow. To grow into a deep knowledge of the Christian faith, and a knowledge of how that received faith can be worked into their own personal theology. To grow through the rings of faith into a fully *owned faith*. To practice their Christianity in a way that not only sustains their personal faith, but that demonstrates to others that they live differently in this world because they follow Jesus. A faith community that can provide that kind of strong holding environment—one strong enough to hold the attention and inspire the commitment of a distracted generation—will have to be one of spiritual maturity. It will have to be a place where Jesus *matters*, and where Jesus can, in fact, be found, when these younger adults go looking for him.

This is not a done deal. We cannot assume that most of our church members are mature Christians, who are grounded in their faith, deeply engaged with the worship, preaching, and teaching of

---

17. Wuthnow, 135.

the church they attend. Many of our churches are filled with people whose faith is primarily *affiliative*, particularly in churches where most of the members are older and come from the generations where church was something you attended for cultural reasons, for business or personal connections, or because the family had *always* belonged to a specific denomination. This means we have an additional task—building committed disciples. Because in order to speak about faith, people have to *have* faith in the first place. This may be the most crucial task for our congregations right now—to build active, joyful participants in the Jesus Movement, and to help all our adult members move from an *affiliative faith* to an *owned faith*.

Some data suggests that this is not happening, across the board. The researchers at Barna Group offer a sobering discovery: "Although people cite their primary reasons for attending church as growing closer to God and learning more about him, Barna Group finds such closeness is a rare occurrence. Fewer than two out of ten churchgoers feel close to God on even a monthly basis. Additionally, while almost two-thirds of those who value church attendance go to learn more about God, fewer than one in ten (6 percent) who have ever been to church say they learned something about God or Jesus the last time they attended. In fact, the majority of people (61 percent) say they did not gain any significant or new insights regarding faith when they last attended."[18]

This is a stunning statistic, that people are attending church without feeling a connection to God and without learning something about God or Jesus. (One wonders why they come at all. . . .) Clearly, we need to awaken the faithful, help them connect to God, and then lead them to a deeper level of spiritual maturity. This is vitally important for all Christians. But it may be particularly crucial

---

18. "Americans Divided on the Importance of Church," Barna Group, March 25, 2014, https://www.barna.com/research/americans-divided-on-the-importance-of-church/ (accessed February 26, 2017).

for post-Boomers, because they are not likely to docilely attend any church that does not inspire or educate. Rachel Held Evans's words hold mainline churches to judgment just as much as they hold evangelical churches to judgment. Post-Boomers will leave the church if they don't find Jesus there.

Furthermore, younger adults are not going to be comfortable in the early circles of the Westerhoff model of faith development. While they might appreciate the acceptance and love of a faith community that is characteristic of *experienced faith*, their distrust of authority, combined with a sense that truth is relative, will mean that they will be suspicious of a "faith community with a clear sense of identity and authority." This will make *affiliative faith* a difficult posture to sustain. The post-Boomers we find in more progressive mainline churches will be far more likely to move quickly into *searching faith*, where doubt and critical judgment take hold, and they can test the community's faith-story and practices.

How a Christian moves from *searching faith* to *owned faith* is important. It is especially important for these post-Boomer generations, which will not rest for long in the early circles of developing faith. These "spiritual tinkerers" need the leadership and guidance of the church, but they will build their own faith that matters uniquely to them if they do not discover their faith awakening and growing in traditional Christian communities. If these Post-Boomers are already in the stage of *searching faith*, then they are coming to ideological consciousness, as Bakhtin outlined it. They need dialogue and conversation. They need other voices to help them distinguish between the authoritative word of everything they have been taught or experienced and the internally persuasive discourse emerging in their own consciousness as they enter into dialogue with others. This is no light task but "an intense interaction, a *struggle* with other internally persuasive discourses."[19] This is the struggle in which post-Boomers

---

19. Bakhtin, 346.

of faith find themselves in this pluralistic, relativistic, secular society. They will need mentors. They will need companions on the way.

In many ways, the Episcopal Church is well equipped to support younger adults on their spiritual pilgrimages. The Episcopal Church affirms and teaches the faith of the ages, while still inviting inquiry and independent thought. To invite post-Boomers into a pilgrim's journey in the Episcopal Church is to invite them into a tradition where they can stand upon the scaffolding of tradition and Scripture as they build their own faith. They can use their reason and experience to construct the kind of personal credo they will insist upon, yet they can ground it upon the teaching of two thousand years of Christianity.

But they will need to do it in dialogue with spiritually mature conversation partners. The strong holding environment that can support people who are moving from *searching faith* to *owned faith* must be a community where a significant number of members—regardless of which generation they are in—have moved to *owned faith* for themselves. A congregation filled with people comfortable in an *affiliative faith* will not be able to support the enquiring and complex spiritual development of post-Boomers.

In faith communities like this—traveling with fellow pilgrims already deeply into their own spiritual journeys, who can act as guides and mentors—post-Boomers can engage in sacred conversations that will strengthen their own foundations of faith. They can learn to identify the Holy in their lives and identify it with the particularly Christian vocabulary and theology that will help them understand and name these experiences as God, Christ, or Spirit working in their lives. They can grow into *owned faith*, come to ideological consciousness, experience true conversion, and learn to *speak their own truth*. If we are willing to travel with them, and to be trustworthy companions on the way.

CHAPTER FIVE

Making a Statement about Faith

As the Speaking Our Faith group gathered for the last time, the sun shone outside the windows, sparkling and dancing on the snow and casting a golden light around the room. Alejandro and Abigail burst into the room with a bag from the local pie shop—the very place they had encountered that 'Holy Spirit moment' with one another. Energy was high as people scurried about, looking for paper plates and forks, then started slurping fruity slices of pie. Mike was late, and when he entered, there was nothing left to eat the pie with but a plastic knife, which he gamely plied to shovel pie toward his mouth.

They had arrived, bringing their final "homework" assignment with them—to create a personal statement of faith based on the Baptismal Covenant from the Book of Common Prayer. This covenant statement, part of the baptismal rite in the Episcopal Church, is divided into two parts: the Apostles' Creed—which describes the nature of the God proclaimed by the church, the God we are in relationship with—and five questions that outline what the

Episcopal Church believes one must do to live a life in relationship with this God.[1]

After pondering the proclamation and questions of the Baptismal Covenant, participants are asked to write their own two-part statement—first, a statement about God and then a statement about how to live in relationship with God. The first part is guided by these questions: "Who is God? What can you say about God, your understanding of who God is . . . today . . . knowing that any description of God can only be partial—and always culturally and personally contextual—but in a description that is YOURS." The second part responds to the questions, "What is required of you as a person in relationship with this God? As a child of this God, or a follower of this God, or as a beloved of this God? What practices, commandments, moral imperatives or commitments does this relationship require of you?"

This assignment is the capstone of all the sessions, the chance for each participant to *speak his or her own truth*, and give voice to the many ideas, questions, clarifications, and images that have been circulating among them during the five weeks of conversation. In the very first session, Cherie had talked about the challenge of saying anything concrete about faith because she wanted to live lovingly and respectfully in a pluralistic society: "It's *so* different growing up where you're constantly talking with people and trying very hard to sincerely value what they're saying and believe, that sometimes when you get down to something as specific as Jesus, all of a sudden you're putting your own markers down and saying, 'Here we are. Here's what I'm saying.'" This

---

1. The five questions are: "Will you continue in the apostles' teaching and fellowship, in the breaking of bread and in the prayers? Will you persevere in resisting evil, and whenever you fall into sin, repent and return to the Lord? Will you proclaim by word and example the Good News of God in Christ? Will you seek and serve Christ in all persons, loving your neighbor as yourself? Will you strive for justice and peace, respecting the dignity of every human being?" (Book of Common Prayer, pp. 304–305)

exercise is the moment to lay down the markers, to commit—at least for this moment—to an understanding of God and the Christian life that is meaningful to that specific person, and that can be proclaimed as a statement of faith to others. After thinking through their own creed and ethics, the participants set down—in black and white—the words and thoughts about God that they can later draw upon when they have conversations with other people about faith. For me, hearing the statement of faith from these courageous conversation partners is always the high point of our time together.

"So you had this little assignment," I said, wiping sugary pie juice off my fingers. "About thinking about God and what your response to God should be, and I wonder how was the experience of actually doing this kind of thinking?"

"It was so much easier than I thought it was going to be," Cherie said. "There's some core stuff that's down here and I'm OK with it and it's good. So, I think this group has helped me get there. If I had written this before, I don't think I would have been in the same place, so thank you to all of you." Blake agreed. "I think from hearing other people share how they mentally worked through their thoughts, it created like a language for me." Abigail said it was a cumulative experience. "Like it was summarizing or crystallizing some of the things I've been saying."

"Were there places where the traditions of our faith were helpful to you?" I asked, "Or places where you struggled with them?" And Alejandro explained that he had interrogated the Apostles' Creed. "I began to think about . . . well, what does this really mean? You know, God the Father Almighty, what does that mean? Magical powers? So I asked more questions and more questions and I feel like I engaged with it. Because of these conversations we've had in this group, I've been able to raise some of these questions." He had become more comfortable with *not having all the answers.*

When I asked who wanted to share their paper, Blake went first, as he typically did, with a confession. "I lost my paper. But I read it before I lost it, so I still thought about the questions." The main points he emphasized were: Being a Christian is about what you do with your faith; nothing is pre-ordained and we have free will; part of faith is wrestling with God; he identifies as a Christian, even though he wrestles with the idea of Jesus; and answering God's call means finding something to do to bring about God's Kingdom.

Mike described God as "the source of all being and all meaning, author of the world, but standing outside and above it. More real and true and beautiful than anything we could hope to be or imagine. God loves each of us so intensely, that God took on human life to participate with us in its joys and despairs, even death and abandonment." And the actions required to be in relationship with this God are: to see each other as God sees us, loving each other. Being mindful of God's presence in prayer and worship. Resist selfishness, exploitation, violence, cynicism and emptiness, and "To share the good news. That the universe is not cold and uncaring, but filled with wonder and love."

Abigail spoke of God as friend and lover, singing over her as she awakes every morning. Of God as Creator, Preserver, Healer, authoring a play that is open to co-creation with the actors. And of God as Graceful Judge, one whose justice might be beyond human comprehension. "There's that law, that principle He governs by that I just don't understand, but in the end, it's about grace." She spoke about required actions as embracing what one must do because of the friendship with God. "And delight and duty is then in the caring of creation, the caring of people, and the healing of people and others."

Kelly struggled—with long pauses and "ummms" between her words. There was a sense that she was unhappy with what she had written, and yet, it was what she believed. God as father, always watching and making sure one behaves a certain way, powerful but full of grace and loving. She cleared her throat. "But yeah, like I said, I feel like my views are very much culturally based, you know?" Required actions are prayer, behaving as God would wish, "you know, loving thy neighbor and being kind and full of grace as much as I can," she laughed nervously, "and forgive as Christ forgave, like I say to my kids all the time." And although she said she felt her statement was very stereotypical, at the end she tackled the second and third commandments and *spoke her own truth* about the exclusivity of God. "I really feel like, ummm . . . that spirituality's important for everyone, and just because I believe in one God doesn't mean that everyone has to believe in that God."

Lisa was typically brief. "Who is God? The force that holds everything and everyone together. The light in the darkness. Pretty much what I got there. What is required from this relationship? To treat others how you want to be treated. Love, kindness, gentleness, understanding. Then understanding that people believe differently from how I do and that doesn't make them any less in God's eyes."

Cherie laid her markers down, and she showed her Sunday school roots by unpacking the Trinity: God as Life Force of unfathomable scope. Jesus connecting divinity to humanity, walking a mile in our shoes to bring us close to the unfathomable God. The Spirit connecting humanity to God and creation. Required actions were all grounded in maintaining a connection to God and creation, a sense of oneness that gave birth to all ethical behavior. "It is this struggle of forging connection and reducing estrangement that lets us build relationship with God, and that is the morality we've been charged with—does it bring us closer to or farther from God?"

Alejandro got a laugh when he said, "I don't have a lot. I spent too much time analyzing this." But he summarized God as both Trinity and Lord of the Universe. And for required actions, he said, "I have a responsibility to pursue a relationship with God," because that leads to more godly relationships with other human beings, and—undergirded by prayer—right behavior can be discerned within the community of faith.

Julia said, "I am in a period of my life where I just feel very confused, and I'll probably get a little emotional about this." And she

was able to describe God as mystery, Jesus as healer and suffering servant, and Holy Spirit as the stagehand putting everything in
play behind the scenes. But then she let herself be *vulnerable* to the
group, and she got tearful as she described her struggles with God
as Father. "A lot of that is because of my own father. So when I think
about God as Father, I think about somebody who's like, waiting to
whack you as soon as he sees like, this chink in your armor." What
is required? Prayer, Sabbath rest, encouraging each other, breaking
bread together, and to "live with integrity, live in a way that's like,
internally congruent."

Natalie spoke of God as a "thing or being that gives me a gentle
cosmic shove in the right direction." She too struggled with the
Father image—because of her own parents, and also because of
her issues with gender concepts. "For me, God is genderless, and I
constantly have to work against culture, and against teachings, and
work even against the Bible." And what's required is what a former
boyfriend told her once: "Love God. Love other people. Don't be
a jerk."

The Power of the Baptismal Covenant

The Baptismal Covenant is a statement of faith that is publicly
renewed every time a person comes before a congregation to be baptized, generally in the regular worship service held on certain important days in the church year: the Baptism of Our Lord, the Easter
Vigil, Pentecost, and All Saints. All the Episcopal members of this
Speaking Our Faith group had become accustomed to proclaiming
this covenant several times a year in worship, at every baptism. For
those from other denominations, it provided a structure they could
use as they constructed their own statements.

Martin Luther, the great Protestant Reformer, began every day of
his life by crossing himself and saying, "*Baptizo sum* (I am baptized)."

For Luther, and also for Episcopalians who are invited to "renew our own Baptismal Covenant" as part of a baptismal liturgy, baptism is not a singular moment of salvation, but a promise, a relationship that needs to be renewed and reclaimed regularly. In offering the Baptismal Covenant as a model for a faith statement, it grounded the group participants' words in our Christian tradition, a tradition that is ancient, yet ever new.

The two-fold pattern of this kind of statement—a description of God and a statement about right relationship with that God—goes all the way back to the original covenant between God and the Israelites, as described in Hebrew Scriptures. There, God and Israel enter into relationship, but it is not a relationship of equals. Because God brought Israel out of slavery in Egypt, Israel accepts God as a suzerain, or sovereign ruler, and agrees to follow the Law, the Torah, the divine guidelines that God sets forth as the right way for Israel to live in relationship. In a divine-human covenant, God acts on our behalf, and we respond to that action.

In the Baptismal Covenant, God's Triune nature and saving action is described in the Apostles' Creed. This ancient theological statement about God's nature, God's work, and God's ongoing life in history arose out of apostolic preaching and early baptismal liturgies. This formal statement about God is followed by the five questions that describe specific Christian behavior and practices. In worship, even though the congregation speaks as one, the response to these questions is not corporate, but individual: "I will, with God's help." Whether renewing the Baptismal Covenant for the hundredth time, or entering it for the first time in baptism, every time that Covenant is spoken, each person must again make the choice of faith, must choose to commit to God and to a new life in Christ. The Baptismal Covenant teaches each Christian—and also teaches the entire Church—that "baptism is not a private religious activity without implications for life in the world," as Leonel Mitchell wrote. "The

Baptismal Covenant commits Christians to living out their baptism in their daily lives."[2]

Using the Baptismal Covenant as the foundation to write a personal statement of faith draws on this great well of tradition. From the Israelites in the wilderness—responding to God's claim on them with a promise to live according to the Law—to twenty-first-century Episcopalians responding to each of those five questions by saying "I will, with God's help," God has used covenantal relationship to draw humanity closer to God, and to guide humanity to live in ways that are authentically coherent to God's dream for a redeemed world. The participants in Speaking Our Faith did not necessarily know how deep this well of tradition goes, but it was there for them, in the two-fold structure of their statements, in the personal creed each had to construct, and in the ethical and behavioral statements they made about how to live out their relationship with God in their daily lives.

To use the Baptismal Covenant in this way also brings participants to the practice of testimony. Of all the questions in the Covenant, the one that people tend to squirm over is the third one: "Will you proclaim by word and example the Good News of God in Christ?" When I work with the questions in baptism preparation classes, invariably someone will share that quote often misattributed to St. Francis: "Speak the Gospel at all times, and if necessary, use words." Meaning, of course, that they don't actually plan to speak any words at all about the Gospel, if they can avoid it.

But coincidentally, saying the Baptismal Covenant out loud in church *is* speaking about God, Jesus, and the Good News—*with words*. So even if people are just speaking the Good News liturgically, in unison with others, straight out of the Prayer Book, they are still speaking about their faith. The Baptismal Covenant is the

---

2. Leonel L. Mitchell and updated by Ruth A. Meyers, *Praying Shapes Believing, A Theological Commentary on the Book of Common Prayer*, revised edition (New York: Seabury Books, 2016), 118.

first step to learning the practice of testimony. And the Baptismal Covenant can also become a springboard to constructing a personal, theological, ethical statement. It can provide guidance for how to "lay down your markers" in a way that is authentic to the person's own faith and ethics.

In some ways, this is similar to the radio and podcast effort called *This I Believe*. In 1951, noted journalist Edward R. Murrow was struggling with his own questions, wondering what he himself believed, and how he was to live. He began a radio program that ran until 1955, which sought statements from renowned thinkers and writers, as well as average people on the street, asking them to distill their guiding principles and values into brief, powerful essays. *This I Believe* featured statements of faith from celebrities like Helen Keller, Eleanor Roosevelt, and Jackie Robinson, along with equally moving essays from cab drivers, businessmen, and secretaries. In the troubled years of the early Cold War, with a nuclear arms race revving up and McCarthyism in full swing, Murrow hoped to help Americans articulate their deeper values, and identify the place of morals and spirituality in their lives. He hoped to help people think about this question for themselves, so that anyone might be able to articulate a *This I Believe* statement.

This I Believe was revived several times, most recently as part of the Public Radio International (PRI) program *Bob Edwards Weekend*, from 2009 to 2014. A nonprofit group was created to support and sustain this effort, providing curricula for teachers, community groups, and faith communities in order to help them lead others in the practice of writing short, three-minute-long testimonials. The creators of the current *This I Believe* iteration believe that writing, reading, and listening to others' statements about faith can help build tolerance and acceptance in a diverse world. Where Cherie was afraid of saying anything about faith in her diverse circle of friends, for fear of offending, *This I Believe* proclaims that making a faith statement is the first place to start building respect in a pluralistic society. Dan

Gediman, one of the program's founding producers, said, "The goal is not to persuade Americans to agree on the same beliefs. Rather, the hope is to encourage people to begin the much more difficult task of developing respect for beliefs different from their own."[3]

So this project of writing a personal statement of faith and reading it out loud in a small group, in a safe space—a statement like the essays of *This I Believe*—can encourage and inspire post-Boomers to build their own capacity to speak about faith. And the work of listening compassionately to each other's statements within the group builds their capacity to listen respectfully to many different ideas about faith when they are outside of the group. It gives them a place to start from when they attempt to speak that faith to their friends and family members who do not share their faith. It can lead them, like it led Blake, to testimony.

Speaking One's Own Truth—Blake's Story

Blake was the "church shopper" assigned to find a new church for his family when he and his wife—"two pro-choice, pro-labor, pro-women's rights Christians," as he put it—no longer felt comfortable in the Catholic Church. But after his family joined an Episcopal church, Blake started to hang back, even as his wife dove right into church membership and church activities. He suffered with debilitating insomnia, and Sunday mornings were often his only time to catch up after a week of nights with only three or four hours of sleep. But much of his hesitancy to get too involved with church life came from his earliest experiences with faith.

Blake's big frame shifted uneasily in his chair, and his almond-shaped, brown eyes gazed down at the table as he told how—in his childhood—he had an intense, evangelical conversion experience.

3. "About *This I Believe*," *This I Believe, A Public Dialogue About Belief—One Essay at a Time*, http://thisibelieve.org/about/ (accessed March 11, 2017).

His agnostic parents did not attend church, but they didn't mind Blake going off with friends to a Baptist church, where he was 'saved.' "At first, it was like an amazing experience. I felt a spiritual experience. I felt connected. I was talking to people. I was worried that everyone I knew who didn't go to church was going to go to hell. It was like this fervor. I'm like seven years old."

But then he went to church camp, where people tried to re-convert him. "Everyone wanted me to be saved, even though I said I had been saved. But they didn't care. They needed as many notches on the belt, and as many times as you wanted, you could re-live this. And it made it feel phony." They also told him his mother was going to hell, because she wasn't going to church. And that put him off Christianity entirely.

Blake describes it with words of shame: "I made a fool of myself. Because I was so excited about this thing called Christianity, and then I came to see it as something like a joke, which made me feel like a joke." These painful feelings return when he feels "the urge to evangelize. That old emotion comes up. I feel like I'm always cautious against that now." These feelings cohere with Brené Brown's definition of shame: *Shame is the intensely painful feeling or experience of believing that we are flawed and therefore unworthy of love and belonging.*[4] The pain of shame can create a deep desire to avoid those painful feelings in the future, so it is to Blake's credit that he came back to Christianity again, slowly, and very much on his own terms.

Given this particular life experience, Blake was amazed that he later decided to speak to his mother about his faith and his time in the group. "Depending how I look at it, she was either the best person or the worst person to pick. There's so much history, and so much background. I would describe my mom as an agnostic who thinks highly of people who go to church. She has no negative feelings about Christianity, she just never attended. The earlier experience I had

---

4. Brown, 69.

was independent of her. She was like, sure if you want to—go with them. She never went."

His father died when he was ten, and Blake said that his mother had been a lifeline for him his whole life. But while she was always tremendously supportive of Blake's re-involvement with church, she never showed any interest in religion herself. When people tried to talk about faith with her, when her own parents were dying and in hospice, she took it very badly, saying, "You want them to do this song and dance at the end? They never believed it in life. You're saying they need to believe this to have their lives validated?" Faith was a touchy topic in their family.

But Blake made an attempt. He was at her house, painting a room, and they spoke for about a half an hour. For the first time, instead of just talking about what went on at church, Blake spoke about his actual religious beliefs, what the group had meant to him, where it had led him. She listened without criticism, but Blake left the conversation feeling bad about himself. He felt bad because he didn't ask his mom about her own thoughts on religion, and he left with no more insight about her faith or lack of faith than he ever had. He also felt bad that he somehow couldn't bring himself to invite her to church. All those old feelings returned, and the same words of shame popped back up as he described this conversation, including the word "foolish," over and over again.

But Blake did not let this experience silence him. Something had shifted for him after the conversation group ended. He took on a major role as a lay worship leader of a Sunday afternoon service. He had also volunteered to coordinate the homilist schedule, and one week, when he could not find a homilist, he stepped up and did it himself. The text was John 4:6-26, Jesus in conversation with the Samaritan woman at the well.

Blake stood there in the small chapel, clutching a few sheets of paper tightly. He read quickly, but earnestly. He began to tell his story, speaking his own truth. He told about participating in the conversation sessions, he told about the conversation with his mother and how hard it was to speak about faith, and he told about his sense that he is not a good spokesperson for Christianity because of his doubts and his dry periods. "Surely," he said, "There are Christians more qualified than me to spread the word."

Then he told about encountering the story of the Samaritan woman, a completely unlikely candidate to speak on behalf of any faith. "Nevertheless, this is the woman that Jesus has sent to deliver his message. One of the things that amazes me is that when she goes to the village, she is still not certain Jesus is the Messiah. Her message boils down to: *here is a man that I met and he might be the Messiah.* She is still not sure but invites everyone to come see for themselves."

Blake blinked as he looked up and around the room, at the sixteen or so people gathered in the candlelight around the communion table. "I find this woman speaking to me today," he said. "She is reminding me that we don't need to be experts in Christianity to spread the Good News, and even in the face of my substantial doubts, I can be a Christian messenger. My prayer for today is that God will allow this woman's story to inspire us to follow the example of this remarkable woman. Through her, Jesus is calling us to spread his word. He does not care who we are. All that matters is that we have had an encounter with Christ, and we are willing to speak with others about our encounter. If we can do this much, Jesus will do the rest."

Testimony—Speaking the Truth about God

When Blake stood before the small congregation that night and talked about the Samaritan woman and our Christian call to speak about our encounters with Jesus, his honesty—his ability to *speak his own truth*—moved into the realm of testimony. Testimony is a way of speaking about God, telling a core truth about who God is, how God has worked in one's life, and how life is to be lived now that God has claimed that person for God's own. For mainline Protestants, testimony is not a common practice, the way it might be in a more evangelical church. But it is part of our heritage, going all the way back to the earliest days of faith.

Long before it emerged as a practice in Christian churches, the practice of testimony was deeply rooted in our own story, the story of scripture. One of the earliest testimonies is found in Deuteronomy 26:5-9:

> A wandering Aramean was my ancestor; he went down into Egypt and lived there as an alien, few in number, and there he became a great nation, mighty and populous. When the Egyptians treated us harshly and afflicted us, by imposing hard labor on us, we cried to the Lord, the God of our ancestors; the Lord heard our voice and saw our affliction, our toil, and our oppression. The Lord brought us out of Egypt with a mighty hand and an outstretched arm, with a terrifying display of power, and with signs and wonders; and he brought us into this place and gave us this land, a land flowing with milk and honey.

This proclamation is a way the Israelites connected to their own salvation history. After they came into the Promised Land, after their enslavement was over, after their journey in the wilderness was over, when they were settled and secure, Israelites were required to remember who God is, and who they were. This statement of faith was to be spoken whenever an Israelite brought the first fruits of a new harvest to be offered to the priest. The first fruit offering was a chance to proclaim again the story of God's deliverance, and to remember that being in relationship with God demands a response. But the statement itself is a declaration about God. It is testimony.

Throughout the Hebrew Scriptures, the repetitive phrase of God as the one "who brought you out of Egypt," becomes a testimony for people, prophets, and kings. It proclaims the saving action of God. It becomes a warrant for how God's people are to behave with one another. It is the way the Lord introduces the Ten Commandments

(Exod. 20:2). It is what parents are to tell their children when the children ask why they must follow all the decrees of the Law (Deut. 6:21). It is the heart of Joshua's long testimony at Shechem, when he challenges the people to "choose this day whom you will serve" (Josh. 24:15). And prophets like Jeremiah and Amos use the testimony of God's deliverance—the one who "brought you up out of Egypt"—to chide and correct the wandering people of God.

The New Testament is filled with testimonies. They are halting, like the words of woman at the well: "[He] told me everything I have ever done! He cannot be the Messiah, can he?" (John 4:29). They are irritable, like the man born blind: "I do not know whether he is a sinner. One thing I do know, that though I was blind, now I see" (John 9:25). They are awe-filled, like Mary Magdalene reporting her encounter with the risen Christ: "I have seen the Lord!" (John 20:18).

After Jesus's resurrection, the testimonies of his followers become more definite, and more deeply grounded in the story of God. Peter's proclamation on Pentecost morning sets the whole story of Jesus's death and resurrection in the Davidic stream of tradition in the Hebrew Scriptures, and he proclaims the truth the disciples are still learning to honor, "This Jesus God raised up, and of that all of us are witnesses" (Acts 2:32). In Acts 26, Paul stands before King Agrippa, relating his whole story of growing up as a strictly observant Jew, then persecuting followers of Jesus of Nazareth, and finally, having a conversion experience on the road to Damascus. "To this day I have had help from God, and so I stand here, testifying to both small and great, saying nothing but what the prophets and Moses said would take place: that the Messiah must suffer, and that, by being the first to rise from the dead, he would proclaim light both to our people and to the Gentiles" (Acts 26:22-23). And the testimony of Paul recorded in the first chapter of 1 Timothy tells the same story, breaking forth, in the end, in sheer doxology: "To the King of the ages, immortal, invisible, the only God, be honor and glory forever and ever. Amen" (1 Tim. 1:17).

After the days of early Christianity, testimony as a church practice declined as Christendom expanded. If everyone in Western society was a Christian by virtue of the dominant culture and infant baptism, the need to make personal statements of faith was less pressing. But after the Protestant Reformation, in some branches of Protestantism, the practice of testimony re-appeared. In fact, in Puritan churches in Colonial America, making a testimony was required to be a church member. One had to come before the community and speak one's own truth about God in a conversion narrative that described how God had saved that person, and what evidence from the person's life could be offered to demonstrate that he or she was saved. Today, testimonies are commonly offered in holiness and evangelical churches by members longing to share their truth about how God has worked in their lives. Even in our own mainline tradition, one can sometimes hear testimonies offered in church. They might be labeled "stewardship minutes" or "ministry minutes." Perhaps they are personal reflections written and offered for a Good Friday service on the Seven Last Words, or short essays for a booklet of devotionals. Even disguised by other names, these personal stories of faith and God stand in this long stream of tradition that is testimony.

Testimony as De-Privileged Speech—A New Way of Speaking

Diana Butler Bass has explored how testimony functions differently in mainline congregations than it does in evangelical settings. As an example, she highlights how the intentional practice of testimony in one United Church of Christ congregation—Church of the Redeemer, in New Haven, Connecticut—"sparked renewal in the congregation . . . the congregation both grew numerically and deepened spiritually—as they created a culture of leadership based on storytelling,"[5] describing testimony as "the most democratic—and empowering—of all Christian practices."[6] Bass says that the testimonies she heard in the thriving mainline congregations she studied were not the formulaic, "I was sunk deep in sin and Jesus took me in," but instead were unique, unrehearsed, deeply personal stories of how God had gotten all involved in a person's life. This kind of testimony, she writes, "is not about God fixing people. Rather, it speaks of God making wholeness out of human woundedness, human incompleteness . . . [it] is not a spirituality of arrival, of the certainty of securing eternal life. Mainline testimony is the act of getting there."[7]

If we are to retrieve the practice of testimony in the Episcopal or other mainline traditions, it will need to be authentic to our spirituality and denominational personalities. The standard evangelical testimony of sin and redemption will not feel comfortable to mainline Christians. Also, in this increasingly pluralistic and secular world, the standard version of testimony—simply proclaiming a truth about God as something to be universally acknowledged, without considering the contexts and cultures and prejudices and ignorance around faith that dominate society today—is going to convince fewer and fewer people. Instead, Old Testament scholar and theologian Walter Brueggemann offers another way of imagining testimony . . . as de-privileged speech, a "bid for assent," rather than a proclamation that assumes a universal consensus. This alternative way of testifying to the truth about God—up from the underside—is the best way forward, he believes, in the new, postmodern world, where the "construal of the world *without reference to God* is intellectually credible

---

5. Diana Butler Bass, *The Practicing Congregation: Imagining a New Old Church* (Herndon, VA: The Alban Institute, 2004), 100.

6. Bass, 2006, 134.

7. *Ibid.*, 141–142.

and socially acceptable as it never has been before in European-American culture."[8]

Brueggemann looks to the kind of testimony offered by ancient Israel in the Hebrew Scriptures for guidance in ways we might speak about God in our secular age. Israel frequently had to speak the truth of God in de-privileged situations far more extreme than the indifference of our own postmodern era—in slavery under Pharaoh or in exile in Babylon. As people that began as nomads and then became exiles, Israelites were never power players, always living under the sway of the big centers of influence in Egypt, Assyria, Babylon, or Persia. And when Israel did speak about its God, Brueggemann notes that the message was one that conflicted with the power of empire. "Israel always comes into the great courtroom of public opinion and disrupts the court in order to tell a tale of reality that does not mesh with the emerging consensus that more powerful people have put together."[9]

When Israel spoke of God under these conditions, it used the genre of testimony. Not testimony in a Calvinist or revivalist manner, but more like a courtroom testimony, where truth is contested and witnesses who may be profoundly contradictory each have a story to tell in the search for the 'truth of the matter.'[10] The Speaking Our Faith participants could be seen as de-privileged witnesses in the courtroom of public opinion about faith. They were aware that *their* construal of God's reality would be measured alongside *other* understandings of reality, each with its own adherents and points of credibility, as Brueggemann describes it. Some of those other statements came from expressions of Christianity that the group members did not want to be identified with. Some of them came from people of

---

8. Walter Brueggemann, *Deep Memory, Exuberant Hope: Contested Truth in a Post-Christian World* (Minneapolis, MN: Fortress Press, 2000), 19.
9. *Ibid.,* 21.
10. *Ibid.,* 20.

other faiths or no faith at all, people whose lives and opinions were sincerely valued by the group members. So as the participants imagined how they might speak to others about faith, each knew him or herself to be one voice among many, one witness for God in a world that has no consensus understanding of God.

It is this de-privileged position that characterizes the Old Testament practice of testimony, Bruggemann writes. Offered by a community of nomads, peasants, and exiles, far from seats of power, Israel tells an outsider's tale that does not mesh with the vision of the powerful. Instead it tells of that strange and irascible Yahweh, who causes barren women to give birth and slaves to be freed, who sends bread from heaven into wilderness hunger, who causes kings to rise and fall, and who cares for the widow, the orphan, and the alien in the land. Israel sometimes offers this testimony to the nations, more often to its children to transmit the faith to a new generation. "Most regularly," Bruggemann writes, "this testimony of alternative truth is offered to members of the community by the community," to sustain and nurture one another in sustaining this contrary vision.[11]

Bruggemann says the risk of this kind of testimony is that it comes as a truth "from below" in the face of a stronger, dominating truth. And in that de-privileged position, it has particular characteristics. It is: *"Fragile.* It depends upon the nerve of the teller. *Local.* It makes no sweeping, universal claim but appeals to what is concretely known. *Persuasive.* The rhetorical casting aims at winning the jury. *Contested.* It dares utterance in the presence of other claims that may be more powerful and more credible. *Fragmented.* It is only a bit of a narrative that brings with it a whole theory of reality that is implied but left unexpressed."[12]

And so when Blake stood to deliver his homily that night, it was from a de-privileged position—as a person plagued with doubts and

---

11. *Ibid.,* 22.
12. *Ibid.,* 21.

dry spells. He identified himself with the Samaritan woman, someone also in a societally de-privileged position, but who was able, nonetheless, to speak her own truth about the man she had encountered, a man who *might* be the Messiah. Blake spoke as a member of the community, to the gathered community, as God's children have done for millennia. He gathered his fragile nerve, told his own concretely local story, aimed to persuade the listeners that all of us could take up this same practice of testimony. He spoke while knowing others were more qualified than he to speak, and then he offered his own fragment of reality for the congregation-jury to ponder.

The Conversation Ends, to Begin Anew

The last session of Speaking Our Faith is often a bittersweet time. As group members courageously offer their statements of faith, they do it knowing that this small community is coming to the end of its life together. Their journey from feeling challenged to speak about faith to being able to deliver their own personal testimony is over. In the process, some move from *searching faith* to *owned faith*. Others still struggle, even while they can see that some of their issues and concerns are coming clear. All of them have become more able to speak about the faith that is in them, even when they are still not sure that their faith is fully formed.

As this particular group finished the process of reading their statements, they began to look at each other with a kind of nostalgia blooming in their eyes. So I asked them what they were able to say about God now that they couldn't have said before the sessions began. Everyone said that the experience had been helpful. Some comments related to *speaking one's own truth*. Blake: "I've learned a vocabulary." Cherie: "I feel a lot more prepared for a conversation about faith, and just going wherever it will go, and I feel confident that I can do that." Mike: "I feel like I've seen a way of talking about faith being modeled, in terms of asking very open-ended questions, and it's made me feel more comfortable with asking questions myself. And I feel like that's a big part of any faith conversation, because it's easy in some ways to say, 'This I believe.' It's sometimes harder to say, 'So what do you believe?' "

Others had become more relaxed about *not having all the answers*. Lisa: "What's been nice is to hear all the doubts people have. It's OK to struggle, because it's through the struggle that we become better." Kelly: "I've looked at it as a journey and to see where people are at various points in their journey has helped me be comfortable where I am." Alejandro: "I feel more comfortable being able to talk about the parts of my faith that are not as clear, that are not as black and white. As a result of being in this group, with our expressions of doubt and expressions of questions and the wrestling with our individual journeys, it has helped me. It has strengthened me a lot to be able to be much more open and honest about my faith with others, rather than just keeping it to myself."

And then I asked, "If you were to say what is the Good News, what is the thing, the one thing you know about God, that makes it all worth it?" Natalie said, "You're not going the wrong way." "God is still speaking," Alejandro said. Julia said, "He is making all things work together for good. You know we don't necessarily know what that good looks like, and it doesn't always maybe feel good every step of the way, but to think that all things in the universe are working for His purpose is pretty cool." Kelly: "We're all where we're supposed to be. Maybe we don't know why, but there's a reason, and that's comforting." Abigail added, "I just know that I am deeply loved. That is what sustains me." Lisa said, "Every day I wake up is a good day, and that's part of that gift from God, finding beauty in the mundane." Blake: "Christian fellowship has healing power." Mike said, "I think two things: One is God's presence and the experience of the presence and knowing that experience has been real in my life. The other is one of the last verses in the Bible, 'Behold, I make all things new.' God is saying—at the very end of things, I'm making it new again, and

whatever happens in our world or to our world, or in our relationships or our lives, that piles up brokenness and ugliness and hurt and
bad things, God can still make it new."

There is one final homework assignment at the end of Speaking
Our Faith, a charge, if you will, as participants head back into their
own lives: *to have a conversation about faith with someone you
already know, but someone you know who does not share your faith.*
This is where the ability of this program to build the capacity for
evangelistic speech is tested. After speaking freely with a small group
of people in a safe space protected by group norms and sustained by
growing trust and familiarity, can participants then move out into
their wider circle of friends and associates as people equipped to
speak about the faith that is in them, and to listen thoughtfully and
respectfully to the faith stories of others? Can they become evangelists, bearers of the Good News of God in Christ?

CHAPTER SIX

Reclaiming Evangelism: Learning to Listen, Learning to Speak

Evangelism has a bad rap in mainline Protestant circles, where it is sometimes coyly referred to as "The 'E' Word." Because it comes with a load of baggage, bad imagery, stereotypes, and clichés: *Saving souls for Jesus. Getting "notches on your belt." Hellfire and brimstone. Witnessing. Handing out tracts. Jehovah's Witnesses at your door. Slick salesmen. Altar calls. The guy holding up John 3:16 signs at football games. TV preachers.* And also because our institutions—Episcopal, Presbyterian, Lutheran, Methodist, UCC—did not position themselves to be evangelical. They were built to sustain the spiritual lives of people already inside. People were certainly welcome if they found their way through our doors, and if they were willing to be re-formed into the denominational mode. But the idea that neighbors, friends, or family members outside the institution needed "saving," needed conversion, or needed to be evangelized, was never a strong aspect of mainline Protestant identity.

Instead, as Mike described it in a conversation after his Speaking Our Faith group ended, "there was a default assumption that you were a Christian in some way, unless you were publicly described as 'other.' If you were from China, if you were Jewish, if you were Arabic, then, OK, we could assume you were not Christian. But otherwise, we assumed you were a Christian." But as Christendom has collapsed, even mainline Protestants can no longer make that assumption. The cultural notion of faith identity is shifting to a more secular understanding. "Now we assume you'll buy presents at Christmas and candy at Easter," he said, "but we don't assume your faith life has any real content, unless you explicitly say so."

Evangelical churches never made that assumption, that the people around them were safely ensconced in some sort of Christian church, which would provide access to eternal salvation. For evangelicals, the salvation stakes are extremely high—you are dealing with someone's eternal future, a future that could be horrifying if that person ends up in hell, condemned to eternal damnation. So it is essential for them to share their faith—whether in a one-on-one conversation, or at a huge, Billy Graham-style revival with an epic altar call. For evangelical Christians, it is not enough for someone to be baptized as an infant and raised in a Sunday school. A person must make an intentional commitment to Jesus, to sign on a dotted line, as it were, to ensure their eternal salvation.

Jenna, a forty-year-old paralegal, participated in a later Speaking Our Faith group, and she found the process helpful as she transitioned from the "save a soul for Jesus" mentality of her childhood faith into the world of mainline Protestantism. Jenna grew up in an evangelical church, where she was taught that every conversation with someone new was an opportunity to bring that person to Jesus. "The idea of talking about your faith was very important, and one I was familiar with. There was always a purpose, and the purpose was converting other people. That was the goal. You were supposed to bring it into the conversation, no matter what, and if you don't, well . . . you really should."

Somewhere in this great divide—between mainline Christians who believe evangelism is rude, tacky, or unnecessary, and evangelical Christians who believe that evangelism is the means by which you are obligated to save countless souls from eternal peril—the word "evangelism" got lost, neutered of its power, and stripped of its real meaning. Reclaiming this word in a way that is authentic to our identity as mainline Christians is necessary, if we are to share our faith with future generations.

What Can Evangelism Mean to Us?

At its core, the word "evangelism" means to proclaim Good News, specifically good news about God's salvation of the world through Jesus Christ. The word comes from the Greek *euaggelion*—*eu*, meaning "good" and *aggelion*, meaning "angel" or "messenger." It's a Good Angel Message, like the one shouted by the heavenly host to the shepherds: "Glory to God in the highest heaven and . . . peace among those whom he favors!" (Luke 2:14). It is often translated as "gospel," as in the Gospels of Matthew, Mark, Luke, and John. It is at the core of the very first verse of the very first gospel ever written—the Gospel of Mark: "The beginning of the good news of Jesus Christ, the Son of God" (Mark 1:1). To evangelize is to proclaim this Good News, to announce it. To be an evangelist is to be a herald, a proclaimer, a town crier.

The relevant promise in the Baptismal Covenant presents evangelism as just this—proclamation. "Will you proclaim by word and example the Good News of God in Christ?" The Episcopal understanding of the word "evangelism" is not salesmanship, or closing a deal, or guilt tripping, or browbeating. It is proclamation, announcing something wonderful, something true, something life-changing.

That God has always been, is at this very moment, and will continue into the future, redeeming and reconciling this broken world. That the life, death, and resurrection of Jesus Christ make this redemption and reconciliation accessible for everyone. That through the action of the Holy Spirit, God is active and involved in the life of the world, bringing light into darkness, hope to erase despair, and transformation where there was stagnation. Jesus Christ came into the world to bring us home to God. The power of God working through Jesus Christ changes lives. Evangelism is proclaiming that truth.

But in order to re-appropriate the word—"evangelism"—in a way that younger, twenty-first-century, mainline Christians can claim it, we have to retrieve its biblical roots. What does it mean to speak "good news" about God? Walter Brueggemann situates his understanding of the word "evangelism" in the three-part movement of God's redemptive drama found in the Bible. "At the center of the act of evangelism is the message announced, a verbal, out-loud assertion of something decisive not known until the moment of utterance."[1] It is speech, it is conversation, and it is words said aloud about God. There is no avoiding this definition. The Good News is not to be intuited from someone's behavior, as Christ-like as that behavior may be. Any Christ-like behavior will still require an explanation that takes it well beyond the putative St. Francis quotation—one may indeed preach the Gospel at all times; however, it is still necessary to use words.

But the verbal proclamation does not exist in a vacuum. There is more to evangelism than telling people, "I have accepted Jesus Christ as my personal Lord and Savior." Brueggemann says the proclamation is the bridge, the hinge point, in a three-level pattern. Or perhaps the second act in a three-act drama. The first act is God's victory— over the forces of evil, corruption, slavery, illness, even the power

---

1. Walter Brueggemann, *Biblical Perspectives on Evangelism: Living in a Three-Storied Universe* (Nashville: Abingdon Press, 1993), 14.

of death. Scripture tells these stories of God's triumph—bringing
Israelites out of Egypt, ending the exile in Babylon, sending Jesus to
heal the sick and proclaim the coming Kingdom of God, raising Jesus
from the dead through the power of Easter that turns even death on
its head, and at the end, winning the ultimate victory of Revelation,
when heaven and earth are reconciled at last, and "the home of God
is among mortals. He will dwell with them; they will be his peoples,
and God himself will be with them; he will wipe every tear from their
eyes. Death will be no more; mourning and crying and pain will be
no more, for the first things have passed away" (Rev. 21:3-4).

God works first. In Scripture, and in human lives. The victory
comes first. Then the second act, the evangelistic act: the proclamation, the announcement, of what God has done and is doing and will
do. Finally, the third act in Brueggemann's drama is "the *lived appropriation* of the new reality now announced."[2] How does life change,
once you have heard the news of what God has done? The result of
the victory, the result of the proclamation, is open-ended and not
guaranteed. It "does not follow automatically from the announcement, easily, readily, or automatically; rather, the appropriation is
difficult, costly, demanding work."[3]

Those of us who are followers of Jesus Christ understand the
challenge of living that appropriation every day of our lives. We are
disciples. And our call is not to "save souls for Jesus." It's to make
more disciples. When the risen Christ gives the Great Commission,
he tells his disciples to "go therefore and make disciples of all nations,
baptizing them in the name of the Father and of the Son and of the
Holy Spirit, and teaching them to obey everything that I have commanded you" (Matt. 28:19). The Great Commission commands us to
make disciples, to lead people who are willing to *be* different and to
live differently, into a new kind of life, where they take on the *lived*

2. *Ibid.*, 30.
3. *Ibid.*, 37.

appropriation of the Good News, the new reality of God. We follow Christ because that lived appropriation means everything to us, because in him we have found a new way of living that sustains us in ways the world cannot. That is the Good News we have to share. That is the new reality we are called to invite others into.

Or, as David Gortner describes it, evangelism is what arises out of the lived appropriation, "of your own transformation. Your message of hope, of abiding faith, of joy—your 'song of love unknown'—can only become natural, free, and open when you recall for yourself those moments of rescue, reorienting, awakening, and invigoration that are the result of God's work within and around you."[4] As each of us becomes more deeply incorporated into God's drama of victory-proclamation-appropriation, the story becomes more and more our own. We have something to say about God. We have Good News to tell.

Learning to Speak and Learning to Listen

This is a conversation we must learn to have because when we can speak about the new reality we discover ourselves living in—evangelism results. Conversation is the route evangelism *must* take, to Brueggemann's mind: "The subject of the evangelical conversation is how our life, our bodies, and our imagination can be weaned from the deathliness of the world to newness of life in the gospel. It is a conversation to which all are invited."[5]

The process of Speaking Our Faith draws people more deeply into God's story through these sacred conversations. Learning to identify and claim where God is at work in one's life. Hearing from others that God is active in their lives, too. Hashing out in dialogue with others, and in reflective exercises between conversations, what one actually believes and can claim. Articulating, at the end, a statement

---

4. Gortner, 2008, 2.
5. Brueggemann, 1993, 46.

of faith—halting and provisional, but also personal and authentic. While five weeks of sacred conversations will not make fully formed evangelists out of anyone, the process does build comfort, competency, and courage in speaking about faith.

"I wouldn't say I feel comfortable talking about faith with other people," Mike explained. "But I feel less UNcomfortable. I always felt like faith was something you did on your own time, and you didn't really share it outside the church. It lived in its own sort of bubble, and you could talk about it inside the bubble, but you didn't take it out of the bubble. But the focus in the group on how you share your faith in a way that is respectful of other people's beliefs, along with your own doubts and misgivings, but that can still show others the joy and grounding and sustaining peace that you find in your faith . . . to me, that was pretty radical."

"I've found myself being more comfortable even saying anything at all," reported Beth, a thirty-four-year-old, stay-at-home mom and part-time youth minister at a local church. Beth was a participant in a later Speaking Our Faith group, who subsequently reflected on her group experience with me. Her childhood had been spent in a very strict non-denominational church, followed by an adult foray through Catholicism, before coming to the Episcopal Church. "By the time I joined the Episcopal Church, I was so conflicted about what I believed. But my group really helped me nail down . . . oh, this is why I believe this. And oh, this is why I feel this way about certain things. And so much has changed since Speaking Our Faith, because now I work for the church. I would not have felt comfortable in this job before. I would have said, 'What do you mean? I can't help teenagers figure out Jesus. I don't know about Jesus myself!' Just the other day I even had a conversation about faith with my plumber, who is a whole other kind of Christian from me, but I was able to have a conversation about faith and not freak out."

The process of sacred conversation also helps to build better listening skills. Many of the participants' initial notion of evangelism was that it meant to talk *at* someone about Jesus. But after five weeks of deeply listening to one another, they came to see that respectful, open-minded listening is just as much a part of the evangelical process as talking. Their understanding of evangelism became more like what Sheryl Kujawa-Holbrook has described as "relational evangelism." This practice involves listening to someone first—before speaking. It means getting to know another person well through hearing his or her stories. Only then does one offer one's own story in turn.[6] Gortner calls it "radical spiritual listening," focusing on the life stories of others, and listening to where God might be at work in their lives, "listening for the spiritual and theological meaning in what people are telling you about their experiences."[7]

Because many post-Boomers in mainline congregations came to these churches from a variety of denominations, listening to other group members with different religious backgrounds or different questions about God can become like a cross-cultural experience. People from evangelical traditions are reworking and reclaiming their Christianity in light of their new understandings of God and how God works in twenty-first-century lives. But those who grew up in mainline Protestant denominations have their own questions about God, and often their own preconceptions about evangelicals, as well. Listening with an open mind as another person wrestles with questions about God can not only build better listening skills—it can also build a deeper level of understanding and compassion for other ways of being a Christian and other ways of believing.

For someone like Alejandro—who found himself the most theologically conservative person in his group—exposure to possibly shocking ideas about God can be a bracing awakening. "Hearing

6. Sheryl A. Kujawa-Holbrook, "Resurrected Lives: Relational Evangelism among Young Adults," *Congregations*, Spring 2010, 17–21.
7. Gortner, 2008, 135.

people who had such a wide range of experiences and theologies was really powerful. It gave me an opportunity to self-reflect," he said. For a "cradle Episcopalian" like Cherie, it might be a brand-new exposure to the theologies and practices of evangelicals. "This was the first time I really understood better—not just in passing—what it means to have an evangelical background, and how that gives you a certain viewpoint on the world and God," she said.

Listening thoughtfully to another's story of faith became such a powerful practice for Alejandro, that his first conversation about faith after Speaking Our Faith ended was with a Muslim friend. He wanted to know honestly what his friend believed and what his Muslim faith meant to him. So Alejandro barely said anything about his own faith. Instead, he used the non-judgmental listening techniques that he had practiced in the group, encouraging his friend to speak about faith, and listening with kind regard to those faith stories—just as he had listened with kind regard to the faith stories of his Speaking Our Faith group members.

And for Cherie, while she still says that she doesn't "evangelize," she admits that she has become a much better listener, willing to meet people where they are, and ready to speak only when the situation warrants it, after listening, when the time is right. "I don't feel like I want to go out and talk *at* people. But now it doesn't feel at all like that. It just feels like when it comes up, I have more real stuff to say. I'm pretty open if people want to talk about stuff and it comes up naturally." And although she says she is not "evangelizing," Cherie is regularly bringing friends from her neighborhood to worship with her at church. Perhaps for some people, speaking about faith can become that comfortable, so that it no longer feels like "evangelism." Perhaps, as Gortner has said, maybe it really can "be as easy as talking about an apple, or bread, or a friend."[8]

---

8. Gortner, 2008, 139–140.

Where to Begin? First Steps in Speaking About Faith

With an increased level of comfort in speaking about faith, with a deeper understanding of what one does and does not believe, with an acceptance of *not having all the answers*, and with some practice in *speaking one's own truth*, Speaking Our Faith participants leave the group with a challenge: have a conversation about faith with someone you know who does not share your faith. The key elements in the challenge are that this attempt is:

1. *a conversation*, a give and take, involving listening as much as speaking,
2. *with someone you know*, not a stranger, but a friend, a family member, a colleague, or a neighbor, and
3. *who does not share your faith*, whether that person belongs to another faith tradition, or has lost their faith, or has never believed.

The most successful conversation starters rely on existing relationships, like, "I have been part of this group at my church, and I have an assignment, will you help me? I need to talk to you about faith." Or "You know our culture is so strange. We talk about so many things, but not faith. Would you talk to me a bit about your relationship with faith?" Approaching a friend, family member, or colleague with a stance of *vulnerability*—of needing help with a conversation about faith, or of wondering honestly about another's faith—can prove to be disarming and inviting.

Sometimes it means listening for the right opening. Lisa, so quiet and shy, was watching television with a friend one day and a news segment on same-sex marriage came on. Lisa's friend knew that Lisa was a lesbian, but not that she was a Christian. And for the first time in their long friendship, Lisa "came out" as a Christian to her friend, explaining that her faith undergirded her support of same-sex marriage, and that she didn't find a conflict between her Christianity and her stance on marriage equality.

This stance of "being out" as a Christian at a workplace or in a group of friends can also provide openings for conversations about faith. To be the only church-goer in a social or workplace setting provides the opportunity to speak, to share, even to defend the faith. Mike has talked to his co-workers about the difference between saying "Merry Christmas" or "Happy Holidays"—"I told them actually it's Advent, so you should save 'Merry Christmas' for the twelve days of Christmas." And when other co-workers asked how he could be comfortable with "what the church says about evolution," he said, "Well, I'm comfortable with what *my* church says about evolution." And the conversation opened up as Mike talked about the differences between progressive Christians and fundamentalist Christians, and their differing approaches to science and scripture. In a polarized political and religious society, being able to represent a tolerant, progressive, mainline approach to faith in a fair and open manner can play a crucial role in reducing tensions around religious belief.

And with an increasing number of people describing themselves as "nones," and those who have a low level of understanding about basic beliefs of Christianity, Christians who are able and willing to explain basic doctrines and practices can also start conversations about faith. Cherie learned that one of her daughter's friends did not know what Easter was. And Cherie was happy to tell the child the Easter story. "I was like, oh, let me try that one, because that's not a weird story to try to explain." She felt it was not a weird story because she had been teaching Sunday school recently, and already telling that story to children. So the words just flew off her lips.

But these kinds of conversations are just initial forays into the practice of speaking about faith. For the sort of dialogues that can mirror the depth and subtlety of the group conversations, a deeper commitment is needed. It might require a longer period of conversation, where there can be deep listening and fruitful give and take. It might need to be a conversation with someone in a long-standing relationship, say a family member or good friend. It might require taking the kind of risks Gortner describes as part of the practice of evangelism—"I will remember my own wonder, joy, and gratitude. I will speak; I will tell my stories. I will meet other people listening for the Holy in their lives."[9] This deeper conversation will be more than simply sharing the teachings and traditions of the Church. It will result in speaking about faith, personal faith, in the same way one might speak in the safety of a Speaking Our Faith group. This deeper level of conversation can be especially helpful, and especially profound, in three particular situations: interfaith dialogue, conversations with unbelieving family members, and authentic evangelical speech.

Speaking of Faith in an Interfaith Context

The number of Americans identifying with a faith other than Christianity is quite small—only 5.9 percent in 2014. But that number grew significantly, up from 4.7 percent in 2007, according to Pew Research Center.[10] Still, their presence in the population is low. So while people in urban areas might regularly encounter Muslims, Jews, Buddhists, and Baha'is among their colleagues and neighbors, people in rural areas and small towns may still find themselves in a unilaterally Christian region. Beth, the newly confident youth minister, grew up in such a small town, and never met someone who practiced another religion until a Jewish family moved to her town when she was in middle school. "I honestly didn't realize that Jewish people still existed," she said. "I thought they were people in the Bible.

---

9. Gortner, 48.

10. Pew Research Center, "How Americans Feel about Religious Groups," July 16, 2014, http://www.pewforum.org/2014/07/16/how-americans-feel-about-religious-groups/ (accessed April 22, 2017).

Then this family moved to my town, and I was like, wait . . . this is still a *thing*?"

This kind of unfamiliarity with the basic tenets of the world's religions can make people of other faiths seem complicated or alien. And the polite flip side—wanting to be "respectful" of another's faith—can result in people not talking about faith at all. But in a time when religious conflicts come home to roost in the form of religiously inspired terrorist acts, or hate crimes aimed against people of a specific faith, and when Americans feel "warmest" toward Jews, Catholics, and Evangelicals, and "coldest" toward Mormons, atheists, and Muslims,[11] interfaith dialogue has never been more important. Religion can be a powerfully divisive force. How we learn to live together in an increasingly diverse nation will be crucial in the years ahead.

While the proportion of people professing a faith other than Christianity is small, it is growing and younger adults especially are more frequently exposed to people of other religions. More than older generations, post-Boomers are more likely to encounter people of other faiths, and are more likely to be converts to other faiths.[12] There are Muslims and Jews, Hindus and Buddhists in their classrooms, their workplaces, and in their social networks. So they will need a level of comfort and competency in speaking about faith that their parents might not have had to bother with. For Jenna, the paralegal who was once a hard-core evangelical, this kind of interfaith speech is important. "One of my son's best friends is Jewish, and another one is Hindu, so it's good for me to be in a place where I can have conversations about faith. They may not be very deep, but it's a different place to be coming from than 'you need to be like us.' It's being able to bring our faith practices to the table the way they bring theirs to the table, and we can talk about that together."

---

11. *Ibid.*
12. Wuthnow, 86, 101.

But the kind of conversations fostered in a Speaking Our Faith group can lay the groundwork for an even deeper kind of conversation about faith across religions—not simply informational exchanges, but real, heartfelt conversations between a faithful Christian and a person of another faith. For young Americans living in an age of religious pluralism, these practices of relational evangelism—of listening deeply and sharing honestly—build compassion and tolerance, says Sheryl Kujawa-Holbrook. "Rather than deny religious difference, relational evangelism equips young adults to be secure enough in talking about their own faith to engage actively and authentically in interreligious dialogue and community action for the common good."[13]

To engage in a deep conversation about faith with someone of a different religion is not an opportunity for proselytizing, but for honest dialogue. Because the practice in a Speaking Our Faith group is to listen without judgment to the struggles and beliefs of others, while still *speaking one's own truth*, younger adults who have participated in Speaking Our Faith will be better equipped for the kind of relational conversation that can foster interfaith understanding. And although such a conversation is not for the purposes of proselytizing, it is still evangelical speech—honest Good News about how God is working in one's life, while listening to someone of another faith tell their honest Good News of how God works through their religious beliefs and practices.

As Speaking Our Faith participants head out to have a conversation about faith with someone they know who does not share their faith, they frequently turn to friends or colleagues who are adherents of other religions. Cherie talked to a childhood friend who was Jewish. Even though they had been friends since fifth grade, they had never really talked about their faith before. "What was fascinating is that ninety-five percent of what we believe and how we experience

---

13. Kujawa-Holbrook, 21.

spirituality and religion is absurdly close," Cherie explained. But there was a difference, based more in how her friend practiced Judaism, than in the ideas they both shared about God. When it came time to talk about how faith functions in difficult times of life, Cherie asked, "When you are stressed at work, or have a bad moment, how do you pray? She was like, no, I don't. So that was really different. It was interesting to see how we think so similarly, but the way it plays out is different."

For her conversation challenge, Abigail turned to her Muslim housemate, a man from Tanzania, who was culturally Muslim from his upbringing, but not very observant. "And he has a huge interest in understanding Christianity because he loves to watch televangelists on TV and he loves Joyce Meyer and T.D. Jakes, so I knew it would be an interesting conversation," Abigail said. As they shared their life stories, they both realized that in high school, each of them—living on opposite sides of the planet from one another—made a decision to believe in God, and particularly in an expansive, loving God. "I told him how I didn't grow up religious, but I made a choice, and I committed to this faith, and I told him how music was part of the process that helped me understand I was worshipping a living God," she said.

And when her friend told her he had read some parts of the Bible, and discovered the concepts of mercy, and repentance, and grace, Abigail explained that for her, Jesus was the model of mercy, and repentance, and grace. "I wanted to be sure that he heard me when I said there's a reason for Christians that the Jesus story is so central to the faith. I wanted to make sure he heard that, and knows that." And when the conversation ended, she felt inspired, "lifted up, really. I think both of us were grateful for the exchange. It was a sisterly and brotherly thing, that's how it felt, that we were embracing each other's differences."

For those brave enough to engage in these kinds of conversations, there is a gift: they discover that even though they might be *vulnerable,* and *don't have all the answers,* but they still want to *speak their own truth* . . . the person they reach out to turns out to be much the same. It is a risk for both parties to talk about something as tender and vulnerable as faith, and to admit that they don't have all of it figured out. It takes courage to be willing enough anyway to take a stab at saying what they do or do not believe. So whatever religion the conversation partners may profess, what they learn by speaking together about their differences is that it's not important if their faith is the same, or their God is the same—what's important is that they, as people of faith, are very, very much the same.

Speaking of Faith to Unbelieving Family Members

It was just a Facebook post. Eliza, a twenty-three-year-old, newly minted French teacher, was in the midst of her Speaking Our Faith group when she posted, asking what people in her network of friends were planning to do for a Lenten discipline. Then her brother private messaged her—*So you're still doing that God thing, huh?* They had both grown up in the same family, with a limited amount of church attendance. In adulthood, her brother had gone the way of the "nones." Eliza instead made a conscious decision to re-engage with a church and with her faith. They had never talked with one another before about the choices they had made or the paths they had taken. But then her brother opened the door (or the Messenger window, really).

In a long series of message bubbles, Eliza tackled the topic. "I told him that I had stepped away, too, but that in college I felt the draw back to church, so I followed it. And I told him why I had chosen to become more active in my faith and what I was getting out of it. I have had some conversations with coworkers about church, but this one with my brother was the first serious one I have had, where it was an actual *thing* kind of conversation."

Speaking about faith with unbelieving family members is one of the bravest and most vulnerable actions a person can do. While one might think that family is the safest place to speak about something that really matters, instead, family often feels like the riskiest place to have that kind of conversation. Family dynamics and old baggage can make it feel like a minefield to begin to have a conversation about faith. And yet, speaking about something so significant with family members—the most important people in your life—can also become an urgent priority. A voice deep inside says that these people—the ones who know you best—should also know this central aspect of your identity.

Kelly—the reticent believer who drew her house of faith as a fortress with a deep moat—didn't plan to have her post-Speaking Our Faith conversation with her mother. But one day, her mother started questioning Kelly about her faith. Why did she go to church? What was going on? "We were together one day, and my mom just got real serious," Kelly said. "It felt like it might be a juxtaposition in our relationship, and I felt like I had to navigate it carefully. She asked me if I've been a believer for a long time, and I said, 'I think I have. I remember praying as a child. So I think it's always been there but now I have the time and courage to kind of explore it and figure it out.'"

Kelly's act of evangelism was small, but true. It fits into Brueggemann's three-part drama of evangelism. Who God is and how God came into Kelly's life happened off-stage, quietly but powerfully enough to convince her to follow Christ. But then the moment came to proclaim God's work in her life, and to live forever after in whatever reality followed that proclamation. Kelly practiced evangelism as Gortner describes it, "Evangelism is naming your own journey to love with the living God, wherever it takes you, and naming the presence of the Holy in the journeys of other people you encounter."[14]

---

14. Gortner, 2008, 34.

They talked a long time, and Kelly's mom was concerned about what she might say to her grandchildren, who are being raised in a Christian home. "My mom was like, 'If they ask me, I'm going to say my beliefs, I'm going to be honest.' Which is scary." But by the end of the conversation, Kelly felt that her mother knew that Kelly did not condemn her for not believing. Then, just a few days after the conversation, Kelly's mom was talking to her granddaughter, Kelly's middle daughter. The little four-year-old was saying something about God, and her grandmother said, "Where is God?" And the granddaughter replied, "You know, Deedee . . . in your heart." Kelly started crying as she told this story. "And my mom is like, 'That makes sense to me. That God's in your heart.' My mom was like, 'I can buy that. You know. Just in your heart.'"

It got tense for Kelly when she exposed herself as a person of Christian faith. She risked an encounter with one of the most influential human beings in her life—the woman who birthed and raised her, an only child with a single mother. And *juxtaposition*, the word Kelly used to describe the moment when her mother asked about Kelly's faith, captures this tension. It was a placing of two things side by side—Kelly's faith and her mother's atheism—and it would reveal whether this relationship would stay the same or suddenly change. That word acknowledged the power of the gospel to disrupt relationships, as Jesus says in Matthew 10:32-36. Acknowledging Christ before others can bring not peace but a sword, can set a daughter against her mother, and can even make foes of the members of one's own household.

Instead, Kelly's risky moment of vulnerability created a connection around this question of faith. The relationship between *this* daughter and *this* mother could bear up under the risk of vulnerability. Brené Brown says, "When it comes to vulnerability, connectivity means sharing our stories with people who have *earned the right to hear them*—people with whom we've cultivated relationships that can bear the weight of our story."[15] Not every relationship with every relative can bear this weight. But family members who have spent decades loving us and who want to have a good relationship with us—even if we have taken a different path of faith—*can* bear that weight of honest vulnerability around our identities as believing Christians. Kelly could describe truthfully where she was on her faith journey, while still empathetically accepting that her mother would be honest about her own lack of faith. And that is a good starting point for a rich conversation about faith with family members who do not believe.

The Great Leap of Faith—Connecting Your Story with Another's Story

In the depth of some of these conversations about faith, a moment happens where space opens for something more—an invitation, or a connection. After deep, compassionate, non-judgmental listening to another, after *speaking one's own truth* about God, sometimes a light shines in to the conversation, and opens up the possibility of extending a deeper invitation into life with God. Gortner calls it "naming the Holy in someone else's life,"[16] a way of hearing both the other person's story, and the simultaneous movement of the Holy Spirit, busily at work in that person's life. And when that moment happens, when that insight dawns, it can take your breath away. It's like standing on the brink of a precipice, knowing that this is an opportunity to connect the dots, to draw the line of connection between that person's story and the movement of the Spirit. And to speak to them about the connection you have discovered. Out loud. With words.

15. Brown, 160.
16. Gortner, 2008, 142.

It feels risky, and dangerous, to move from a conversational stance of 'this is my own truth about God, and I accept wherever you are with God,' to 'I wonder if God is speaking to us right now, and if together, we can hear God's voice and respond?' This is the final, fruitful movement of evangelical speech. It's not proselytizing, because proselytizing is an effort to convince someone that your way of believing is the correct way. It's not a church growth strategy, either, because the Spirit may not necessarily be calling that person to join your church. It is simply this: an honest, true, and vulnerable offer, to say that God might have something to contribute in this person's life.

Some Speaking Our Faith participants leave the group simply with a higher level of confidence, feeling like Mike did, "less UNcomfortable" talking about God and faith. But others have been able to take the leap of faith into evangelism. Some have been able to invite another person to consider that God is real, and that God might have something important to offer that person.

Alejandro stumbled into just such a moment shortly after his Speaking Our Faith group ended. "I have this friend, and we were going to a basketball game, and she told me this really, really hard thing that was happening in her life. And normally, I never would have said anything about God. I don't want to be imposing and telling her she's going to hell or something. That felt like the evangelism I knew growing up." Instead, he listened to her for a long time. He let her talk it all out. Then he said, "I know this is a really horrible time for you, and would you allow me to pray for you? I can't say it's a magic solution. I don't think all your problems will be solved if I pray for you. But I believe prayer connects us to God, and it connects us to each other."

And his friend said yes, absolutely. And they prayed together. "It was just a moment where we were able to connect to God, regardless of what else was going to happen in her spiritual journey," he said. This encounter shifted Alejandro's whole approach to talking about faith with his friends. He no longer worried that he was supposed to convince them that Christianity was true. Instead, he began to offer his faith as a free gift.

"When I know that people are going through really hard situations, I just say, 'Let me be there for you. That's what it means to be a Christian. I'm going to be there for you, and I'm going to listen, and I'm going to pray for you.' And if they don't have faith or they aren't religious in a formal way, that's OK too, because I'm not trying to sell them on anything. I just want them to know I'm here for them, as an expression of my faith. And maybe it will help, if I ask if I can pray for them."

This was a new understanding for Alejandro, whose youth was spent in proselytizing, focused on making converts, even making certain quotas of converts. And maybe this kind of new understanding can also help "God's shy people" become more comfortable with evangelism. It seems startling, maybe even too easy, but it is possible. Evangelism can happen like this, like an offer with no strings attached, just bringing the love of God softly into another person's life. Offering to pray *for* someone. Asking to pray *with* someone. Standing *with* someone and telling them why, like Alejandro did: "That's what it means to be a Christian. I'm going to be there for you."

"It doesn't feel like I'm imposing, and it doesn't feel like I'm trying to change peoples' lives," Alejandro said, "because ultimately, I don't believe I *am* changing peoples' lives. I believe God changes peoples' lives. So breaking out of those notions of what evangelism is supposed to be, breaking away from those fixed notions and pushing forward with what God has done in my life, and what this community of Christians has done in my life, has let me relax so that the Spirit can really do the rest."

Relax and let the Spirit do the rest. That's what Gortner recommends. "At our best, we permit the Holy Spirit to take the lead, trusting that God is already at work in all people, allowing ourselves the possibility of being transformed by new encounters of God's grace among people who do not know the name of Jesus."[17] Imagine the kind of joy we could experience if we could just rest in that place— where God is already at work in all people, and where we ourselves become transformed every time we encounter God's grace at work in people who do not share our faith. We would discover for ourselves the connection that Alejandro talked about, the deep knowledge that we are connected to God, and to these other people, through the working of the Spirit. We would experience love, and a sense of the Holy, and awe, wonder, gratitude, and blessing.

The Carrot or the Stick? Rethinking the Work of Evangelism

When Jesus appears on the scene in the Gospel of Mark, he comes proclaiming Good News: "The time is fulfilled and the kingdom of God has come near" (Mark 1:15a). God is on the move, and Jesus's ministry inaugurates this new way of living, a way in harmony with God's intentions, a way of love, justice, and peace. This is the evangelical proclamation, the announcement of God's saving action.

Unfortunately, Christianity has made a hash of the next state-ment out of Jesus's lips: "Repent, and believe in the good news" (Mark 1:15b). The command to repent indicates clearly that something needs to be relinquished. There needs to be a repentance of all that has kept a person from living a Kingdom of God life. This is not a bad thing. The word repentance—in Greek, *metanoia*—means to turn around and go another way. It means you are headed in the wrong direction, away from God, and you need to turn about and come home to God. Eugene Peterson's translation *The Message* makes it clearer: "Time's up! God's kingdom is here. Change your lives and believe the Message" (Mark 1:15 *The Message*).

---

17. Gortner, 2008, 41, 42.

There is nothing in that word "repent" that means potential punishment, or shame, or chest beating. But over the millennia, this word "repent" became associated with exactly that—potential punishment, shame, and chest beating. "To repent" meant to decide to avoid the fires of hell by believing in Jesus. Thus, for a long time in Western Christianity, the standard evangelical model was the old "carrot and stick": the carrot of eternal salvation and right relationship with God, combined with the stick—the threat of eternal damnation.

However, the "stick" no longer plays well in American society, which has become increasingly secular, tolerant, and pluralistic. The push for greater justice and equality in society—for African Americans, women, LGBTQ people, non-believers, or followers of other faiths—has created a parallel sense of justice and equality in people's religious understandings. Why should God eternally condemn the sorts of people that a growing majority of the American public sees as worthy of equal treatment and respect? Eternal damnation no longer makes sense to many people. It is losing its motivational power.

So if the "stick" of eternal damnation no longer motivates secularized, interfaith, postmodern, twenty-first-century Americans, Christian evangelism will have to try another tactic. It will have to focus instead on the "carrot": the promise of joy, resurrection life, and the sense of life's purpose that comes when one becomes a follower of Jesus Christ. People will want to know the truth of God's redeeming love—not that *I am so bad, and I need to be saved from eternal condemnation.* But *I am loved. I am connected. I have a purpose in my life. I was put here for a reason. I am not alone. My struggles will be redeemed. God is with me, and wants to transform me into the person God created me to be.*

However, even though post-Boomers increasingly reject the "stick," getting to the "carrot" is still going to take some doing. Taboos against publicly speaking about faith are still strong, emphasized by both the wider secular culture, and also by denominations that have neglected to foster and teach evangelism. The growth of the Evangelical movement crushes any desire among mainline Protestants to evangelize, because they fear becoming identified with that aspect of Christianity. And the influences of our secular, postmodern, multifaith culture also deter any desire in post-Boomers to evangelize. The forces Flory and Miller identified—deep skepticism of institutions, wide tolerance of other faiths, rapid global access to a variety of ideas and "truths," and a sense that all truth is relative[18]— make it hard to find a place to take a stand. Post-Boomers want to accept their peers of other faiths, or no faith at all, without insisting that eternal salvation depends on whether or not they are Christian. So even trying to say that Christianity is true can seem like a closed-minded and judgmental statement to them.

The internal challenges of evangelism are also powerful, and may be even more difficult to identify and address, when the topic of faith is so personal and private. Speaking Our Faith participants have either observed or personally experienced the ways that Christianity can be used as a club: Kelly's father telling her that her mother was going to hell for being an atheist; Natalie's neighbors saying, "What church would *have you?*"; Lisa's religious school training that presented an almost bi-polar God who was either "nice like Jesus" or about to punish her for sinning. Add to this the potential shame of being judged by other believers and found wanting, or the shame of possibly being identified as a judgmental Christian, or the shame of being exposed as a person of faith, when that faith was deep and tender, unspoken, and often unformed—it all creates a sense of profound *vulnerability* when it comes to speaking of faith.

When Gortner describes the evangelical process, he emphasizes that it begins in remembering joy and gratitude, speaking and telling stories of that gratitude, then meeting people and listening for the

---

18. Flory and Miller, 2008.

Holy in their lives.[19] This kind of evangelism honors *vulnerability*, and relies upon it. But to build the shame resilience that can allow these faithful post-Boomers, with their questioning, idiosyncratic spirituality, to remain vulnerable, they will need to do their remembering of joy and gratitude together, with one another, in sacred conversations. The faith communities where they have found spiritual connection are where these conversations need to happen. And this is why evangelistic speech must lead to an invitation to join such a community. Gortner warns that you can't view a specific church—with its building, people, and programs—as a promised land. Instead, he says, a church must become a refuge, a way station, a spiritual outfitter that can support and strengthen Christians who are on their own pilgrimages through life. The invitation of evangelism can then be not "join my church—it's so cool," but "come with us on a journey to learn and experience more on the Way, to see God with others who are seeking."[20]

To support faithful post-Boomers, these faith communities will have to be filled with members who have a mature faith, an *owned faith*, as Westerhoff described it. These fellow spiritual travelers, who are already deep into their own pilgrimages of faith, can act as guides and mentors for post-Boomers who are learning to, in essence, evangelize themselves. Conversations will help the process. By talking it through, listening to one another and also to the movement of the Holy Spirit binding them into the Body of Christ, they can become, as Gortner describes, evangelists "like the early Christians, who were passionate about Jesus, flexible in translating the gospel to meet people where they were, open to the Holy Spirit's transformation in their lives, committing themselves to the living God, willing to go

---

19. Gortner, 2008, 48.
20. *Ibid.*, 149.

anywhere people gathered . . . and engaging in personal conversations regularly with others."[21]

The church is already taking its trust fall into the arms of the next generations, the faithful post-Boomers. What they will do with the church, or with Christian faith apart from institutional churches, is still unseen; the church is still falling into the future. We can only share our faith with them as we know it, and help them to give voice to the faith already alive within them. What happens next is veiled from us, as Walter Brueggemann writes: "In every generation, the transmission of the blessing is not only problematic, but laden with mystery. The process of transmission into the next generation is not fully accomplished through human intentionality. Thus, Isaac comes late to his blessing . . . I find these stories important models for our own intergenerational work. They affirm to us that the arrival of the blessing is well beyond our control. One cannot dictate the shape of faith to the next generation . . . there is a freighted mystery between the generations which cannot be penetrated."[22]

---

21. *Ibid.*, 49, 50.
22. Brueggemann, 1993, 108, 109.